U.S. History: People and Events 1865–Present

Author: George Lee
Consultants: Schyrlet Cameron and Suzanne Myers
Editor: Mary Dieterich
Proofreaders: Cindy Neisen and Margaret Brown

COPYRIGHT © 2017 Mark Twain Media, Inc.

ISBN 978-1-62223-644-2

Printing No. CD-404265

Mark Twain Media, Inc., Publishers
Distributed by Carson-Dellosa Publishing LLC

Table of Contents

Introduction

When studying history, students are surrounded by informational text. They must have the ability to understand its purpose, gather key ideas and details, make inferences, and evaluate the information. The goal of this book is twofold: to help students learn about important people and events in U.S. history and to practice informational text comprehension skills.

There are 42 lessons in *U.S. History: People and Events 1865–Present.* Each lesson includes a reading selection and an activity. Each lesson can be used independently or can be combined with other lessons into a unit of study.

Reading Selections

Decisions—we make them all the time. However, we don't usually think of them as being important; in fact, many are not. But the consequences of our decisions can be far-reaching. Decisions made by one person often affect others as well. Some decisions have affected not only individuals and those with whom they come in contact but have changed history. Most of the time, the person making the decision was thinking about himself or herself and what was to his or her advantage at that moment. He or she was not thinking in terms of how people hundreds of years from then would react to it. Some decisions turn out for the better, some for the worse. At times, there were surprising side effects. Eli Whitney's cotton gin is a good example. He was not thinking about how it would create a new demand for slaves. He was only interested in helping farmers clean seeds from their cotton.

As students read the selections, they need to realize that people of the past were products of their time and place, just as we are. We may not approve of things they did, but we cannot judge them by the standards of our time. We can't imagine any intelligent person thinking slaveholding is fine, so we assume they must have felt guilty for owning human property. However, if they grew up in the South before the Civil War, slavery was part of their society, and they may never have met a person who opposed slavery. No one asked what slaves wanted, but eventually some African-American men and women were able to make decisions affecting themselves and history. Fighting duels was another sign of the times, but it wasn't much different than the death-defying risks some people take today. The role of women was much more restricted than in the modern world. Men thought that women were there to cook, tend the garden, and produce children. They thought it was a waste of time to educate women or listen to them. As a result, a woman's role was very limited in making major decisions that affected the nation. Nevertheless, some women made or began making major historical breakthroughs.

Reading Activities

The activities in *U.S. History: People and Events 1865–Present* evaluate and extend the reader's comprehension by:

1. promoting thoughtful consideration of the text;
2. supporting the reader's comprehension with online experiences;
3. checking the reader's comprehension;
4. extending the reader's understanding of the text;
5. identifying the influence or impact of an event;
6. analyzing and explaining the relationship between people, events, and ideas;
7. analyzing primary and secondary sources; and
8. integrating visual information (i.e., photos, maps) with text.

Introduction (cont.)

Reading Comprehension Skills

Reading comprehension refers to a wide range of skills readers use to get meaning from text. While these skills develop over time, the activities in this book provide practice and reinforcement in the following skills:

- stating central idea
- stating main ideas
- identifying supporting details
- citing textual evidence
- making inferences
- following directions
- locating references
- recalling information
- summarizing or paraphrasing ideas
- recognizing text features
- determining word meaning
- identifying text structures
- distinguishing facts from opinions
- conducting research
- categorizing information
- identifying cause and effect
- making comparisons
- identifying the 5 W's

U.S. History: People and Events 1865–Present has been correlated to Common Core State Standards and other current state, national, and Canadian provincial standards. Visit www. carsondellosa.com to search and view its correlations.

Time Line

We tell the story of our lives by dates. Dates also help us understand history. By dates, we can look at the past and see the order in which events occurred. They also help us keep historical events in sequence. This time line covers events from 1865 to the present.

1865	President Lincoln assassinated, Johnson replaces him; Reconstruction begins; Thirteenth Amendment ratified; Freedmen's Bureau created
1866	Civil Rights Act; Atlantic cable laid
1867	Reconstruction Acts; Alaska purchased from Russia
1868	Fourteenth Amendment ratified; President Johnson impeached but acquitted by the Senate
1869	Transcontinental railroad completed
1870	Fifteenth Amendment ratified
1873	Credit Mobilier scandal; the Panic of 1873
1875	Civil Rights Act
1876	Indian Wars; Custer's Last Stand; Telephone invented
1877	Reconstruction ends
1881	President Garfield assassinated, Arthur replaces him
1882	Chinese Exclusion Act
1886	American Federation of Labor formed; Haymarket Riot
1887	Interstate Commerce Act
1890	Sherman Anti-Trust Act
1893	Panic of 1893
1896	*Plessy v. Ferguson*
1898	Spanish-American War; Philippines and Hawaii annexed
1901	President McKinley assassinated, Theodore Roosevelt replaces him
1903	Wright brothers make first flight
1908	First Model T produced
1910	NAACP organized
1912	Wilson elected president
1913	Sixteenth Amendment ratified; Seventeenth Amendment ratified; Federal Reserve created
1914	World War I begins in Europe; Panama Canal completed
1915	*Lusitania* sunk; First full-length movie, *Birth of a Nation*
1917	U.S. enters World War I
1918	World War I ends
1919	Senate defeats League of Nations; Eighteenth Amendment ratified
1920	Nineteenth Amendment ratified
1922	Mussolini's Fascists come into power in Italy
1923	President Harding dies, Coolidge replaces him
1927	Lindbergh's non-stop flight from New York to Paris
1929	Stock market crash; Beginning of the Great Depression
1932	Bonus March; Franklin Roosevelt elected president
1933	New Deal programs begin; Hitler's Nazis come to power in Germany
1935	Social Security Act and WPA established
1938	Munich Conference
1939	World War II breaks out in Europe
1940	Russia seizes the Baltic Republics; U.S. begins the draft; German *blitzkrieg*
1941	Pearl Harbor; United States enters World War II
1944	Normandy Invasion; the GI Bill passed

Time Line (cont.)

1945	President Franklin Roosevelt dies, Truman replaces him; United Nations organized; Atomic bombs dropped; World War II ends
1947	Truman Doctrine; Taft-Hartley Act
1948	Marshall Plan; Berlin Airlift
1949	NATO organized; West Germany formed
1950–1953	Korean War
1952	U.S. tests first hydrogen bomb; Eisenhower elected president
1954	*Brown v. Board of Education of Topeka*
1955	Montgomery bus boycott
1957	Civil Rights Act; Little Rock desegregation; *Sputnik I*
1960	Kennedy elected president
1961	Bay of Pigs; Peace Corps begins; Allen Shepard first American in space
1962	Cuban Missile Crisis
1963	March on Washington; President Kennedy assassinated, Johnson replaces him
1964	Civil Rights Act; beginning of the War on Poverty
1965	Voting Rights Act; Malcolm X assassinated; War in Vietnam expands
1968	Martin Luther King, Jr., and Robert Kennedy assassinated; Nixon elected president
1969	First manned landing on the moon
1970	Kent State riot; Environmental Protection Agency (EPA) created
1972	Watergate break-in; SALT I Nuclear Arms Treaty
1973	U.S. troops withdrawn from Vietnam; Vice President Agnew resigns
1974	President Nixon resigns, Ford replaces him
1976	America celebrates Bicentennial; Carter elected president
1978	Israeli-Egyptian peace accords signed at Camp David
1979	Three Mile Island nuclear power plant accident
1980	Reagan elected president
1981	First woman appointed to the Supreme Court (Sandra Day O'Connor)
1984	AIDS virus discovered
1985	President Reagan and Soviet leader Mikhail Gorbachev meet for summit talks
1988	George H. W. Bush elected president; U.S. troops invade Panama
1989	Berlin Wall torn down; *Exxon Valdez* oil tanker disaster in Alaska
1990	Former Soviet-bloc countries become independent
1991	Persian Gulf War
1992	Clinton elected president; Los Angeles riots
1993	Explosion at World Trade Center in New York City
1995	Oklahoma City bombing
1998	President Clinton impeached but acquitted by the Senate
2000	Mapping of human genome completed; George W. Bush elected president
2001	September 11th terrorist attacks; U.S. troops invade Afghanistan
2003	U.S. troops invade Iraq
2005	Hurricane Katrina devastates the Gulf States
2008	Obama elected president; Economic collapse
2010	Affordable Care Act
2010–2013	"Arab Spring"
2012	Pentagon begins permanently assigning women to battalions
2016	Hillary Clinton is first woman to be presidential nominee of a major political party; Donald Trump elected president

America Faces New Challenges

Victory Parade

In 1865 after the Civil War was over, the Union Army staged the Grand Review of the Armies, a two-day parade lasting 15 hours featuring 150,000 victorious soldiers marching 60 abreast down Pennsylvania Avenue. Civil War losses were staggering: 618,000 killed and many thousands more wounded. Most who marched and watched did not realize how much America had changed during the war.

> **Quick Fact**
>
> Approximately 25,000 horses took part in the Grand Review Parade.

A Changing Nation

Jefferson had dreamed of a nation where independent farmers and craftsmen worked for themselves, but the new America was a land of factories and stores, with people working for employers and not for themselves. Cities were growing rapidly, and farmers worried that their sons and daughters might leave the land to find a job in the city. Skilled labor had been important before the war, but now machines produced goods faster and cheaper than workers could.

Another casualty of the war was the slave system. Lincoln's Emancipation Proclamation of 1863 freed slaves in those regions still in Confederate hands, and wherever the Union Army marched, a long line of former slaves followed. Slaves in the Border States were freed by the Thirteenth Amendment, passed in 1865.

The former slaves (now called freedmen) were the focus of much attention. Abolitionists like Thaddeus Stevens thought freedmen should have the full rights of any citizen, but many in the North and South were sure they were not ready to vote, hold public office, or sit on a jury.

Soldiers Return Home

The Southern soldier, half-starved and half-clothed, began to find his way home. As he walked past charred houses and fields overgrown with weeds, he joined civilian refugees who were almost afraid to return home. Everything had been lost: slaves, money, property, perhaps even an arm or leg. The future looked grim. In some parts of the South, bummers (Union Army deserters) and Confederate deserters went wherever they wanted and took whatever they wanted from anyone they chose. No sheriffs, no courts, and no jails stood in their way. Unless order was restored soon, there was no hope for the law-abiding citizens in the South.

The Northern soldier had better prospects after the war, but he also faced an uncertain future. He was entering the job market at the same time millions of other soldiers were. Where should he go, and what should he do? He might try gold mining in Colorado, working on a cattle ranch, starting a business, working in a factory, or working on a railroad construction crew. He knew the government was not going to take care of him, and he would have to make it on his own.

New Opportunities

During the war, the government had opened new opportunities for expansion. It had chartered two companies to build a railroad to the Pacific, and it had passed the Homestead Act (1862), allowing 160 acres of free land to a settler who improved it over a five-year period. By making the tariff on foreign goods high, manufacturing interests grew.

Name: _____ Date: _____

America Faces New Challenges: Activity

Directions: Use information from the reading selection to complete the graphic organizer.

Independent Farmers

Former Slaves

Explain the challenges faced by each group of Americans after the Civil War.

Northern Soldiers

Southern Soldiers

President Andrew Johnson Is Impeached

Andrew Johnson

Andrew Johnson Becomes President

After President Abraham Lincoln's death on April 15, 1865, the nation went into a time of mourning. Andrew Johnson, the vice president, took the oath of office and became the nation's seventeenth president. Like Lincoln, he had been born poor. His mother had apprenticed him to a tailor, who treated him cruelly. He had run away to Tennessee where he opened his own tailor shop, got married, and learned to read and write. A strong Democrat, Johnson moved up the political ladder, from alderman to United States senator. When Tennessee left the Union, Johnson remained in the Senate. After the Union Army moved into Tennessee, Lincoln appointed Johnson military governor. In 1864, he was chosen for vice president in order to win support from border-state Democrats.

Trouble for Johnson

When Lincoln died, Johnson took the oath of office. He had climbed far since his boyhood, but he never forgot his humble origins. He talked about following a hard line toward the South, which appealed to the radical Republicans in Congress. Their leader, Thaddeus Stevens from Pennsylvania, hated the rich slave owners and blamed them for the war. When Stevens saw Johnson following Lincoln's lenient policies, he turned against the president.

Johnson wanted poor white Southerners to take over in their states, but Stevens was concerned about protecting the rights of former slaves. Johnson opposed the Freedmen's Bureau and the Civil Rights Bill, and he urged states to reject the Fourteenth Amendment. In 1866, Johnson went around the North, on his "swing around the circle" speaking campaign, urging voters to elect Democrats. He was often heckled and probably hurt the candidates he supported. When the opponents were elected, they had a two-thirds majority in both houses and could override his vetoes.

Congress began limiting presidential power. On March 3, 1867, the Tenure of Office Act was enacted. It said the president could not remove a Cabinet member he had appointed without the consent of the Senate. Secretary of War Edwin Stanton cooperated more with the radicals than with Johnson. Johnson waited until Congress adjourned, then fired Stanton. Johnson appointed General Grant as interim (acting) secretary of war. When Congress met, they voted in favor of Stanton, so Grant resigned.

Johnson Is Impeached

On February 24, 1868, the House voted 126–47 that Johnson be impeached, and 11 charges were written by a committee chaired by Stevens. Impeachment trials take place in the Senate. The Constitution requires a two-thirds vote to remove an official from office. It also states that when the president is on trial, the Chief Justice presides. There were 54 senators at the time, 42 of whom were Republicans. All 12 Democrats and seven Republicans voted in favor of the president. The motion to remove Johnson from office failed by a single vote. Johnson finished his term and later returned to the Senate. None of the seven Republicans who voted for him were elected to any office again. Congress had flexed its muscle, and that reminded future presidents for many years that it did not pay to antagonize the legislature.

Name: _____ Date: _____

President Andrew Johnson Is Impeached: Activity

Directions: Complete the graphic organizer by listing the impact of each event. Support your answers with details from the reading selection.

Event	Impact

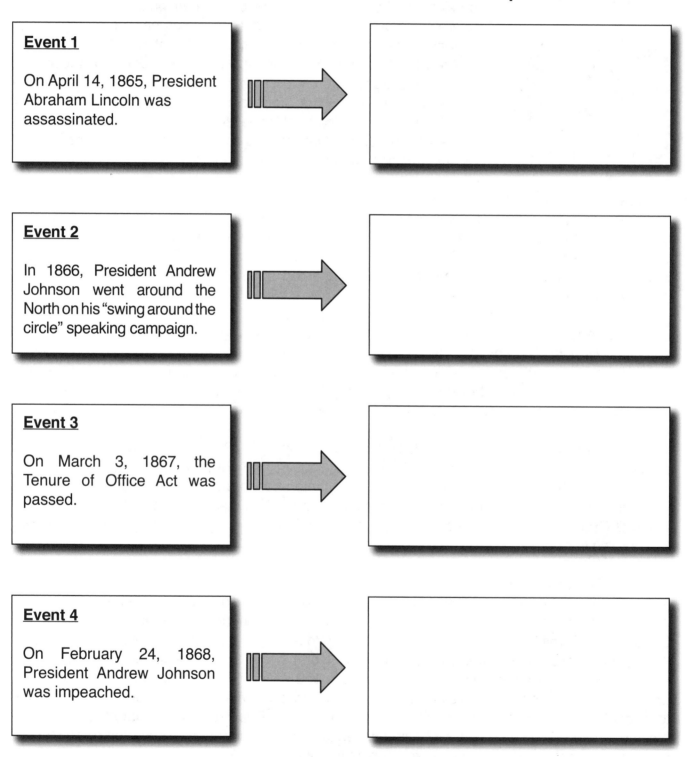

Event 1

On April 14, 1865, President Abraham Lincoln was assassinated.

Event 2

In 1866, President Andrew Johnson went around the North on his "swing around the circle" speaking campaign.

Event 3

On March 3, 1867, the Tenure of Office Act was passed.

Event 4

On February 24, 1868, President Andrew Johnson was impeached.

Reconstruction in the South

The rebuilding of the South after the Civil War posed several challenges. Lincoln developed a plan for dealing with rebuilding the South, called Reconstruction. The plan included:
- housing, clothing, and feeding the millions of freed slaves;
- rebuilding the economy of the South; and
- uniting the Southern and Northern states under one government.

Freedmen's Bureau

"The day of jubilee" had come when the slaves were freed. There were some things they knew they wanted: to reunite with their families, to get an education, and to enjoy the fruits of freedom. The Reconstruction plan established the Freedmen's Bureau to help former slaves. The Bureau provided food, clothing, fuel, and more than 4,000 schools. Students from 5 to 90 years old attended the schools. These schools ran seven days a week, with classes from early morning to late at night. Trade schools like Hampton Institute in Virginia opened to prepare freedmen for skilled labor jobs, but there were also colleges established like Howard University in Washington, D.C., Atlanta University, and Fisk University in Nashville.

South Forms New Governments

As part of the Reconstruction plan, elections were held in the South, and state governments were soon reestablished. The new lawmakers passed laws called the "Black Codes," restricting what former slaves could do and the kinds of jobs they could take. Many Southerners who had served in the Confederate Army were elected to high positions in the states and to Congress. It seemed to Northerners that the South was defying them.

Congress's Plan

Members of the United States Congress were upset with the new governments of the Southern states. So they replaced Lincoln's plan for reconstruction with a new one known as Radical Reconstruction. Under the new plan, the Congress began to pass laws to protect freedmen and establish new state governments. They passed the Fourteenth Amendment (adopted in 1868). It declared all persons born or naturalized in the United States to be citizens. No state could pass a law abridging the rights of citizens; no state could deprive a person of life, liberty, or property; nor deny a person equal protection under the law. They also passed the Fifteenth Amendment (adopted in 1870) that declared no citizen could be denied the right to vote because of color or race.

The new plan divided the ten Southern states into five military districts, each under a general. New voter lists that included freedmen were to be prepared. New constitutional conventions were to be called, this time including black delegates.

Working with the freedmen were two groups: carpetbaggers (Northerners who had moved South since the war) and scalawags (Southerners who worked with Northerners in Reconstruction governments). Together, they wrote laws funding railroad construction, building public schools, and improving local government.

What Were the Results?

Reconstruction legislation helped rebuild the nation after the Civil War. The legislation funded railroad construction and the building of public schools. About 700,000 African Americans were given the vote by the Reconstruction Act, and the Fifteenth Amendment guaranteed that vote. But opposition by Southerners made it increasingly dangerous for African Americans to exercise their right to vote. Government efforts provided little security in the rural South.

Name: _____ Date: _____

Reconstruction in the South: Activity

Directions: Complete the graphic organizer using information from the reading selection. Identify the three main problems the nation faced after the Civil War. Then explain the solutions lawmakers implemented to solve the problems.

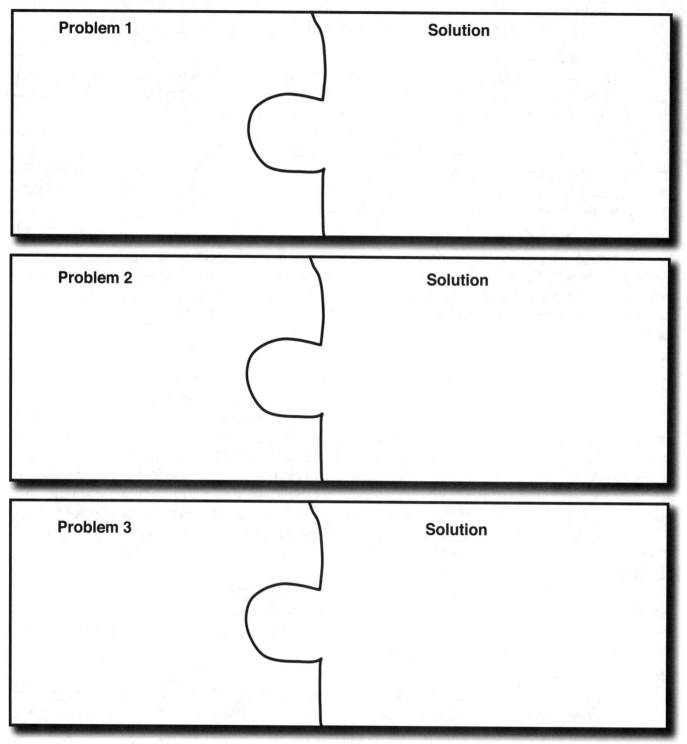

Problem 1   **Solution**

Problem 2   **Solution**

Problem 3   **Solution**

Corruption in Government

Ulysses S. Grant

As the 1876 election approached, one scandal after another was reported in the nation's newspapers. Some scandals were at the local level, like the charges that the Democratic Party's Tweed Ring had corrupted New York City politics. A cartoonist for the *New York Times,* Thomas Nast, drew many pictures of two New York democrats, William Tweed, known as "Boss" Tweed, and Governor Samuel Tilden, who sent Tweed to jail. Many other local governments had their crooks as well. Some went into politics to make money rather than going into business.

Ulysses S. Grant Elected President

The national government was also infected with corruption. In 1868, General Ulysses S. Grant was elected president. An honest man, he did not understand how dishonest men operated. While entertaining him, they would try to convince him that what they were doing was for the nation's good. They pressured honest government officials, who either quit or were removed by Grant. In 1872, the Liberal Republicans tried to dump Grant, but he won the nomination and easily defeated the Democratic nominee, Horace Greeley. Newspapers reported one scandal after another. Democrats were sure they could win the next election and, in 1876, nominated Governor Samuel Tilden for president.

Rutherford B. Hayes Becomes President

Grant wanted to be nominated for a third term, but the party chose Governor Rutherford B. Hayes of Ohio. He was honest, a Civil War veteran, and had no scandal attached to his name. With candidates like Tilden and Hayes, it could have been a clean campaign that dealt with issues they agreed on, like civil service reform and ending Reconstruction. However, their supporters turned to dirty tactics. Republicans reminded the public that rebels (former Confederates) were Democrats, and a Democrat had shot Lincoln. Democrats falsely accused Hayes of taking the pay due dead soldiers in his regiment during the Civil War. Each side used parades, bands, and picnics to gain the people's support.

When the election returns came in, it appeared that Tilden had won; but there were serious questions about whether the vote reported in some southern states was an accurate count. One electoral vote in Oregon was also questioned. Hayes would win 185–184 if all these votes were his. The truth was that both parties in these southern elections were guilty of cheating; it was a question of which cheater deserved to win. Republicans controlled the U.S. Senate, and Democrats controlled the U.S. House, so Congress was divided evenly, and tempers were hot.

The solution found was to set up an Electoral Count Commission (1877) composed of 15 members, with five members each from the House, Senate, and Supreme Court. Eight of these were Republicans and seven were Democrats. They examined the returns and decided by 8–7 in every case for Hayes.

After much arguing, Congress realized they had to set politics aside. If inauguration day came and there was no president, it would create a situation that no one wanted. Hayes was accepted on March 2, 1877, and inaugurated on March 5. He ended Reconstruction and withdrew federal troops from the South. Southern states ended "carpetbag" government, and Democrats returned to power in the South.

Name: _____ Date: _____

Corruption in Government: Activity

A **political cartoon** is a cartoon or comic strip created to communicate a social or political message. It is a way for cartoonists to express an opinion about a topic.

Directions: Go online to <http://loc.gov/pictures/resource/cph.3g05606/>. Examine the political cartoon. Use your observations to fill in each box.

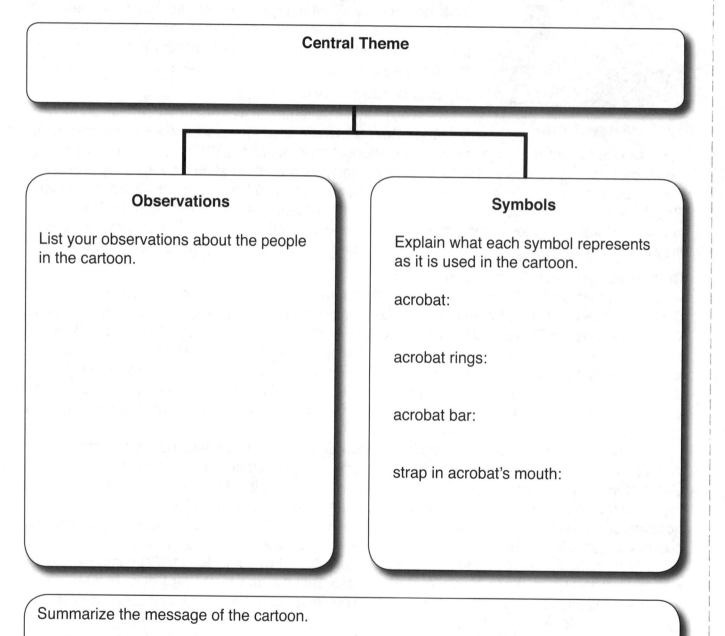

Central Theme

Observations

List your observations about the people in the cartoon.

Symbols

Explain what each symbol represents as it is used in the cartoon.

acrobat:

acrobat rings:

acrobat bar:

strap in acrobat's mouth:

Summarize the message of the cartoon.

The Transcontinental Railroad

Legend tells of John Henry, "a steel-driving man," who built railroads with his sledgehammer and his mighty arms. Americans in the mid-nineteenth century admired railroads. Mayors dreamed of the day the railroad would come to their town and bring in trade, industry, and new settlers. After the Civil War, mayors got their wishes. In 1830, the United States had 23 miles of track; in 1850, it had 9,000 miles; and in 1860, over 30,000. However, nearly all of the railroads were east of the Mississippi River, and the West needed them too.

Steam Locomotive

After the Civil War, "John Henrys" were needed everywhere. The South's railroads were either rusted or Union soldiers had wrapped the rails around trees (called Sherman neckties). During the war, Northern railroads had so much traffic that they now needed new roadbeds, new bridges, and new steel rails. Small railroads were connected into new longer railroads. Commodore Vanderbilt's New York Central expanded from New York City to Chicago. Jay Gould expanded the Erie Railroad from Cleveland to St. Louis.

The Nation Invests in a Transcontinental Railroad

It was not this railroad expansion that attracted the nation's attention, however. It was construction across the plains and mountains to California. The idea had been around for many years, and Abraham Lincoln was enthusiastic about it. The Republican platform in 1860 called for a railroad to the Pacific, and in 1862, Congress chartered two companies to build it. The Union Pacific was to build west from Omaha, Nebraska, and the Central Pacific would build east from Sacramento, California. Very little construction took place until after the Civil War, when many ex-soldiers were available. To add manpower, the Central Pacific brought in Chinese laborers, and the Union Pacific imported Irish workers. The two companies were in a race, and whoever laid the most track got the most government subsidies and land.

In charge of building the Union Pacific was Colonel Grenville Dodge, who understood the land they were crossing, the men who worked for him, and the problems of supply and organization. At first, all supplies came by boat up the Missouri River, but building moved quickly across the Great Plains. Construction of the Central Pacific began more slowly because workers had a harder time getting supplies, and they were soon blocked by the snowy Sierra Nevadas. Once past those mountains, however, they moved quickly, and in one day laid ten miles of track. The two rail lines were joined near Ogden, Utah, at Promontory Point on May 10, 1869.

Each used a construction company. The Union Pacific used Credit Mobilier and the Central Pacific used the Contract and Finance Company. Both companies made huge profits at the expense of the railroads and, in effect, were robbing the government and railroad stockholders. When the Credit Mobilier scandal broke, it showed that stock had been sold at a low price to the vice president of the United States and some important members of Congress.

The nation was connected from coast to coast by rails and not just the Union and Central Pacific railroad to California. Congress also chartered the Northern Pacific (1864), Atlantic & Pacific (1866), and Texas & Pacific (1871). Along with state-chartered railroads, they carried cattle and wheat from the West and brought in new settlers.

Name: _____ Date: _____

The Transcontinental Railroad: Activity

Directions: Examine the illustration. Use your observations to complete the chart. Then answer the question. For a closer view of the illustration, go online to:

<https://commons.wikimedia.org/wiki/File:Chinese_railroad_workers_sierra_nevada.jpg>

Sketch by Joseph Becker. Created in 1869 and originally printed in Frank Leslie's Illustrated Newspaper *on February 6, 1870.*

List people, objects, and activities observed in the photograph.		
People	**Objects**	**Activities**

Based on the reading selection and your observations above, what can you infer about this illustration? Write your answer in the box.

Cattlemen Take Over the West's Rangeland

Cattle Come to the New World

The first cattle came to the New World with Columbus in 1493, and Cortes brought them into Mexico in 1521. Coronado brought cattle into what became the United States, but none of them survived. In 1691, another herd was brought in, and this time, remnants of the herd remained. The cattle adapted to their new conditions and gradually developed the characteristics of the longhorns. With a normal span of horns three to six feet across, these animals came in all colors from white to black. They were able to withstand long periods with very little food and water. Longhorns were easily provoked, and some cowboys said they would prefer facing a bear to an angry longhorn. Without fences or owners, cattle roamed free.

Early Cattle Ranches

Some cattle ranches existed before the Civil War, but there was little market for the longhorns. A few long drives brought Texas cattle to Missouri over the Sedalia Trail. In June of 1853 when farmers saw their cattle suffer from a disease called Texas fever, they stopped the drives. Then the war came, and many Texans joined the Confederate Army. After the war, with unmarked cattle (mavericks) roaming the range, returning soldiers looking for a fresh start, and government land available, the range cattle business grew rapidly.

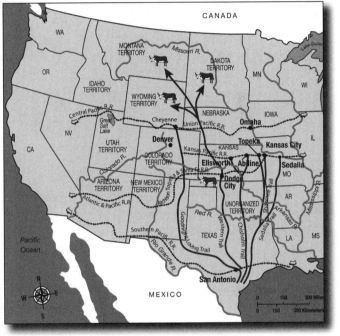

Cattle Trails in the West

Cattle Trails and Ranches

After the Civil War, it was Joseph McCoy who found a way to get cattle to market. He made arrangements with the Kansas Pacific Railroad to ship cattle from Kansas to eastern markets and chose the town of Abilene as his end of trail. Texas herds would be driven north over the Chisholm Trail through Indian Territory (Oklahoma) to Kansas, fattening on the grass as they moved. In 1867, the first herds of Texas cattle headed north, and a new era began.

There were many ranches, but the largest was the XIT. The ranch consisted of 3,000,000 acres of land in the Texas Panhandle and was home to 160,000 head of cattle. Charles Goodnight's JA Ranch in Texas was a 1,000,000-acre spread. The Goodnight-Loving Trail that was used in the 1860s to bring Texas longhorns to market was named after him and Oliver Loving.

What Were the Results?

The cattleman was not alone on the plains, and soon he began to lose control. Sheepmen brought large herds of "woollies" to the plains, and sometimes bitter range wars developed. Homesteaders were also coming, stringing barbed wire across land and putting up windmills to provide their families with water. Most devastating of all were the great blizzards of 1886 and 1887 that killed millions of cattle.

Name: _____ Date: _____

Cattle Take Over the West's Rangeland: Activity

Texas ranchers hired cowboys to drive herds northward to railroads where the cattle would be shipped out to eastern markets.

Directions: Research cowboy life during cattle drives. Using the information, write a letter home. From the perspective of a young cowboy, describe hardships and experiences you encountered driving cattle along the trail.

Custer's Last Stand

George Armstrong Custer

With his long yellow hair and his goatee, George Armstrong Custer was an impressive man. In the summer of 1876, he was eager for an opportunity to make a reputation for himself, and it came on a June day of that year.

George Armstrong Custer

Custer graduated from West Point at the bottom of his class in 1861, but he won many honors during the Civil War and ended the war as a major general of volunteers at the age of 23. After the war, he was reduced in rank to captain. When the Seventh Cavalry was formed, he commanded it and was promoted to lieutenant colonel. He participated in several attacks on Native Americans, including the Battle of the Washita.

In 1874, he led 1,200 soldiers into the Black Hills of the Dakota Territory to disprove rumors that gold was there. However, his men discovered gold, and more miners came into the region, which angered the Sioux tribe. He was then called to Washington, where he testified against the secretary of war before a Congressional committee. President Grant was so angry with him that Custer was removed from his command and was replaced by General Alfred Terry, the district commander. Public criticism forced Grant to back down.

Little Bighorn

In 1876, so many Native Americans had left the reservations that the government ordered them to return by February 1. Instead of going back, many headed for the camp Sitting Bull and Crazy Horse had established on the Little Bighorn River in the Montana Territory. When the army saw that the Native Americans had defied their order, they sent three columns of soldiers to round them up. These were under the command of General George Crook, General Alfred Terry, and Colonel John Gibbon. Custer and his men were under Terry's command. Much effort was involved in locating exactly where the Native Americans were. Once started, the three commanders were out of touch with each other, so Terry did not know about Crook's battle with the Sioux at the Rosebud River. The victorious Sioux then joined with other Sioux, Cheyenne, and Arapaho gathered at the Little Bighorn.

Custer's Last Stand

On June 22, 1876, Custer's 655 men were ordered to search for Native Americans in the Little Bighorn region. Custer was offered Gatling guns (rapid-firing guns mounted on wheel carriages), but he turned the offer down because the guns would slow him down and often didn't work. When they came upon a path almost a mile wide with the tracks of Native American horses, Custer did not follow orders and send for reinforcements. Instead, on June 25, he divided his men into three columns—one under Major Marcus Reno, one under Captain Fred Benteen, and his own column of 265 men. These units were widely separated and unable to do much to support each other. Reno's command came under fierce attack and took up a defensive position on a bluff. Benteen's men joined them, and they were able to hold off attacks. The main attack was on Custer, and he and all of his 265 men were killed. Custer had always dreamed of glory, and while he did find his place in history at the Little Bighorn, his final battle was anything but glorious.

The Native Americans had won a victory, but they knew it was only a matter of time before they would be rounded up and sent back to the reservation. Sitting Bull and many of the others at the Little Bighorn were later killed at Wounded Knee Creek in 1890.

Name: _____ Date: _____

Custer's Last Stand: Activity

Directions: Answer each question about Custer's Last Stand with information from the reading selection.

Who was there?	

What happened?	

When did it happen?	

Where did it happen?	

Why did it happen?	

18

Sodbusters Invade the Great Plains

Wagons crossing the Great Plains sometimes met wagons returning with a slogan on the side: "In God we trusted—in Kansas we busted." For the farmers who worked their claims on the Great Plains, success was not easily come by. Some settlement occurred in eastern Kansas and Nebraska, but it was not until after 1865 that most "sodbusters" went west.

Acquiring Land in the West

There were various ways to acquire land. Government land could be purchased outright for $1.25 an acre under the Pre-Emption Act of 1841. Land could be bought from a railroad, a land speculator, or a state. The Homestead Act of 1862 stated that a person who paid a $10 claim fee and resided on and improved 160 acres of land received title to it after five years. The Timber Culture Act of 1873 gave another 160 acres, providing one-fourth was planted in trees. In 1877, the Desert Land Act gave title to 640 acres to those irrigating part of it within three years.

Farming and Living on the Great Plains

The Great Plains region is different from the area east of the Missouri River. It has little rainfall, and much of its moisture is lost by evaporation. Hot days and high winds might destroy a ripening crop. Without protection from cattle, a field of grain could be destroyed by a passing herd. The lack of trees made it difficult to supply wood for construction, fences, and firewood. The weather on the Plains discouraged settlers: fierce blizzards, rains in the spring, and hot weather in summer made life miserable. Grasshoppers sometimes came in clouds that blotted out the sun and ate everything except metal when they landed.

Without technology, the region could have never developed as it did. Pre-Civil War inventions included Cyrus McCormick's reaper invented in 1834 and John Deere's steel plow in 1837. After the war, many new devices came out to make farm production easier. Without the railroads crossing the Plains, there was little transportation available. Then came two more inventions that were especially useful on the Great Plains. Barbed wire was invented in 1874 by Joseph Glidden, who twisted strands of wire with barbs at intervals. Fencing had never been possible in the West, but now it could be done at a reasonable expense. The more barbed wire was produced, the less it cost. Windmills brought water from deep in the ground to the surface. They were too expensive for many farmers at first, but by the 1890s, they dotted the horizons in most American agricultural regions.

Life was hard for the sodbuster. Without trees, he could not build the usual home, so he dug a cave out of the side of a hill, dug a hole in the ground, or cut prairie sod and built a sod house. These types of homes were warm, but a mouse or snake might drop in on the family dinner. A rain left drops of mud on the table and water pouring across the dirt floor.

What Were the Results?

Many were lured west by misleading advertisements; some stayed, but others had neither the will nor finances to remain. Kansas went from a population of 107,000 in 1860 to 1.4 million in 1890; Nebraska from 28,000 to over 1,000,000; and North Dakota from less than 5,000 to 348,000. At times there was prosperity, but in the 1890s, times turned hard.

Name: _____ Date: _____

Sodbusters Invade the Great Plains: Activity

Directions: Go online to the URL <https://www.youtube.com/watch?v=fdsCjtky6ZQ>. Watch the video about sod houses; then answer the questions.

1. Why did settlers of the Plains build sod houses?

   _____

   _____

   _____

   _____

   _____

2. What were the advantages and the disadvantages of living in a sod house?

Advantages	Disadvantages

3. How did the video contribute to your understanding of the reading selection?

   _____

   _____

   _____

   _____

Growth of Business and Labor Unions

Industrial Revolution

Before the Civil War, a few large manufacturers existed, but after the war there was a great growth in technology, which changed the way goods were manufactured. This time of transition to new manufacturing processes is known as the Industrial Revolution.

America had abundant supplies of most resources needed to become an industrial giant: coal, iron ore, petroleum, and copper, along with agricultural products like corn, wheat, cotton, wool, etc. Technology developed to make these goods into new useful products. Steel replaced iron. Communications improved with a new Atlantic telegraph cable and Alexander Graham Bell's invention of the telephone. The refrigerator car made meatpacking a major industry.

With goods being mass-produced, prices dropped, and consumers were always looking for bargains. Department stores first appeared before the Civil War, but they became more common in cities afterward. In rural areas, people looked forward to receiving their Sears, Roebuck or Montgomery Ward catalogs to buy the same clothes and supplies available in cities.

Captains of Industry

In post-Civil War America, power was not in the hands of the man on the street or even elected officials but in the hands of business leaders. Rich and powerful businessmen were referred to as "captains of industry" (if you admired them) or "robber barons" (if you opposed them). The captain of the steel industry was Andrew Carnegie. John D. Rockefeller owned the Standard Oil Company and was considered a captain of the oil industry. Gustavus Franklin Swift was a leader in meatpacking. Jay Gould became a multi-millionaire in railroading.

The United States had no experience with large corporations; so at first, government saw no need to interfere with the way they conducted business. This was called the *laissez faire* policy, from the French phrase meaning "let someone do as they please." As some corporations got larger, the goal was to create a monopoly. The reason for a monopoly was to eliminate all competition.

Labor Movement

In the years after the Civil War, freed slaves migrated to the cities, most of which were in the North, looking for work. At the same time, immigrants came in large numbers from Italy, Russia, Poland, and China, and even though many of the newcomers could not speak or write English, they were able to fill unskilled labor jobs. Employers showed little interest in their welfare, and some workers decided that only by joining together and forming a labor union could they get attention. The unions fought for better wages, reasonable hours, and safer working conditions.

Several unions formed during the late 1800s, such as the National Labor Union (NLU) and the Knights of Labor. These organizations fought for the rights of the workers. Early unions engaged in violent activities, and soon membership fell off. Samuel Gompers, the leader of the American Federation of Labor (AFL), saw the mistakes of other labor movements and avoided many of them. Under his leadership, the AFL grew.

The management of companies used several tools to fight unions. The *injunction* was a court order forbidding a strike. The *yellow dog contract* was a promise signed by the workers that they would not join a union. A *lockout* closed the plant during a labor disturbance. *Company towns* were used by some employers to house their workers. In case of a strike, they still had to pay rent. Workers were at a disadvantage when they argued with employers, and unions were weak until the 1930s.

Name: _____ Date: _____

Growth of Business and Labor Unions: Activity

Directions: Use information from the reading selection to complete the graphic organizer. Provide the main idea and supporting details for each section heading.

Industrial Revolution

Main Idea:

Key Details:

Captains of Industry

Main Idea:

Key Details:

Growth of Business
and Labor Unions

Labor Movement

Main Idea:

Key Details:

Jim Crow Laws

When most people think of segregation, they think of the South and the African-American struggle to overthrow the "Jim Crow" system that kept blacks from using the same schools, parks, and drinking fountains as whites did. However, segregation started in the North before the Civil War, and the South adopted it.

Booker T. Washington

Right to Vote

The Fourteenth Amendment said that states could not deny any person equal protection under the law. The Fifteenth Amendment allowed African-American men to vote. Before segregation began, black men were already losing the right to vote. This was done through subtle means to avoid having trouble with the federal government and the Supreme Court. Literacy tests, poll taxes, and long periods of residency were required before a person could vote. Literacy was unfairly tested, with harder questions depending on a person's race. Poll taxes were usually $1 or $2 and were collected months before the election. Sometimes polling places would be moved to locations far away from where African Americans lived, or registration for voting was only during short times of the month. Since there were few Republicans in the South, voting in the Democratic primary was more important than the November election. Southern Democrats passed rules preventing African Americans from voting in their primaries. Without the vote, African Americans could do little to stop states from passing Jim Crow (segregation) laws.

Jim Crow Laws

At the end of Reconstruction in 1877, the first Jim Crow laws required racial separation in public transportation: streetcars, railroad coaches, and waiting rooms. Then African Americans were barred from using white barbershops, theaters, and restaurants. Separate schools and state hospitals were built for African Americans. This was a slow process, and different states did it at faster or slower paces. For African Americans who openly opposed the changes, there were segregated prisons and chain gangs. They lived in fear of violent white racists and worried that they were soon going to be losing their jobs or their lives.

Booker T. Washington

In 1895, the Atlanta Exposition was held, and Booker T. Washington of Alabama's Tuskegee Institute was asked to give a speech. Washington firmly believed in the work ethic and saw trade education, hard work, and clean living as the way for African Americans to gain respect. In his speech, he said, "In all things purely social we can be as separate as the five fingers, yet one as the hand in all things essential to mutual progress." Publicly, he did not speak out against segregation, but he quietly sent money to pay for lawsuits to overthrow it.

In 1896, the case of *Plessy v. Ferguson* went to the Supreme Court. The majority ruled that segregation was permissible if facilities were "separate but equal." Justice John Harlan strongly dissented: "The arbitrary separation of citizens, on the basis of race ... cannot be justified on any legal grounds."

Name: _____ Date: _____

Jim Crow Laws: Activity

Directions: Complete the graphic organizer with information from the reading selection.

Central Idea

↓

Right to Vote

Main Idea:

Two Details:

1. _____

2. _____

↓

Jim Crow Laws

Main Idea:

Two Details:

1. _____

2. _____

↓

Booker T. Washington

Main Idea:

Two Details:

1. _____

2. _____

"Remember the *Maine*"

William McKinley

The United States, which had from its beginning shown little interest in the rest of the world, was coming out of its shell in the 1890s. Perhaps it was because imperialistic nations in Europe were grabbing colonies in Africa and Asia. With colonies, there came the benefits of raw materials and a market for surplus products.

Some Americans felt that if we were to take our proper place as a great nation, we must compete for colonies, too. Captain Alfred Mahan of the U.S. Naval Academy wrote *The Influence of Sea Power Upon History,* which argued the need for bases in distant parts of the globe.

Others argued that it was our duty to help the less fortunate people of the world. Cuba and Hawaii attracted American interest. In 1848 and 1854, the United States tried to buy Cuba, but the Spanish refused to sell. The Cubans staged occasional revolts against Spanish rule, but these always failed. American sugar growers had strong economic influence in Hawaii, but the government was in the hands of Queen Liliuokalani. In 1893, Americans in Hawaii tried to overthrow the queen, but President Cleveland sided with her, and it was not until 1898 that the United States annexed Hawaii.

Shift Toward Expansionism

Four events in 1895 caused a shift toward expansionism. The Venezuelan Boundary Dispute over the boundary between British Guiana and Venezuela aroused a strong feeling among many Americans that the Monroe Doctrine must be enforced; some even favored war with England over it. The issue was resolved by compromise. Revolt broke out in Cuba again. At the same time, William Randolph Hearst bought the New York *Journal*, and Joseph Pulitzer bought the New York *World,* and both began to feature stories about Spanish atrocities in Cuba.

To protect American property in Cuba, President McKinley sent the battleship the U.S.S. *Maine* to Havana. On February 15, 1898, the ship exploded. No evidence has ever been uncovered to suggest the Spanish were responsible, but U.S. public opinion blamed Spain anyway. McKinley tried to avoid war by getting the Spanish to end their harsh rule; but when they refused his terms, McKinley bowed to public opinion and asked for a declaration of war.

The Navy was first to act. Admiral George Dewey attacked Manila Bay in the Philippines and won an easy victory. Admiral William Sampson cornered the Spanish fleet in Santiago Harbor in Cuba, and when they attempted to escape, he smashed them with a stunning defeat. No wonder John Hay wrote: "It has been a splendid little war." The U.S. Army was unprepared for war, and its most spectacular unit, the Rough Riders, was a volunteer unit formed by Theodore Roosevelt. Made up of college students and cowboys, their most famous action was capturing San Juan Hill (Cuba). When the peace treaty was signed, the Army had not yet arrived in the Philippines.

The Teller Amendment, passed at the beginning of the war, promised Cuba its independence after the war. In 1901, the promise was carried out. The United States also gained possession of Puerto Rico, and it still remains a U.S. territory today. The Philippines were purchased from Spain for $20 million. After World War II, the country was given its independence.

Name: _____ Date: _____

"Remember the *Maine*": Activity

Directions: Complete the graphic organizer by describing four events in 1895 that caused America to shift toward expansionism. Use information from the reading selection to support your answers.

Causes

Event 1

Event 2

Event 3

Effect:
In 1895, America shifted toward expansionism

Event 4

Theodore Roosevelt Becomes President

At the age of 42, Theodore Roosevelt had accomplished more than most men would ever dare to dream. He had overcome his childhood frailty with bodybuilding, had interests in every subject from art to zoology, had been a New York state senator, Civil Service commissioner, cowboy, police commissioner, assistant secretary of the Navy, and colonel of the Rough Riders. The son of wealthy parents, he took an interest in the conditions of tenement dwellers working in sweatshops. As Civil Service commissioner, he demanded that the tests given to federal employees be practical for the job they were to fill. As police commissioner, he fired policemen for sleeping on the job or drinking at saloons. As the Navy's second man, he sent orders to Admiral Dewey to attack Manila Bay if the United States and Spain went to war. He had thrilled the nation with his charge up San Juan Hill in Cuba.

Roosevelt Becomes President

In 1899, Roosevelt became governor of New York, and in 1900, the Republican Convention strongly backed Roosevelt for vice president. Even though he was not enthusiastic about the job, Roosevelt gave in to public pressure. Since the Republican presidential candidate, William McKinley, was in good health, it appeared that there was little chance for Roosevelt to ever inherit the presidency, and for the first time in his life, he was bored. Then on September 6, 1901, President McKinley was shot by an anarchist and died eight days later. After Roosevelt took the oath of office, Mark Hanna, McKinley's political advisor, remarked, the ". . . cowboy has become President of the United States." In 1904, Roosevelt was reelected president.

> **Quick Fact**
>
> Teddy Roosevelt is one of four presidents sculpted on the face of Mount Rushmore in South Dakota.

Roosevelt's Domestic Policy

Roosevelt used the presidency as a "bully pulpit." It gave him an opportunity to speak out on issues important to him, and he often acted on matters even when he had no authority. Roosevelt and his supporters were called Progressives. They were determined to bring needed reform to the nation by regulating or setting rules for business, transportation, and banking. In 1902, coal miners in Pennsylvania went out on strike, and Roosevelt intervened. He halted the strike and got workers a 10 percent increase in pay. President Roosevelt said he was giving the workers a "square deal," and that phrase stuck.

Roosevelt's Foreign Policy

Theodore Roosevelt was convinced the United States deserved to play a major role in world affairs. He believed to get things done America should "speak softly and carry a big stick." This meant that the nation should try to achieve its aims quietly but be prepared to use force if necessary. He used this strategy to get the Panama Canal built. Roosevelt wanted to build a canal through the Isthmus of Panama, shortening the distance that ships had to travel to pass between the Atlantic and Pacific Oceans. On November 3, 1903, a revolution broke out in Panama City, and the American cruiser *Nashville* was ordered to block the landing of any troops within 50 miles of Panama. On November 6, the U.S. recognized Panama's independence. Panama then gave the United States the right to build the canal.

Roosevelt believed one way a nation could project power was with a strong navy. In 1907, he sent 16 new battleships of the Atlantic Fleet on a world tour. Painted white, the fleet was nicknamed the "Great White Fleet." With this demonstration of strength, Roosevelt paved the way for future U.S involvement in world affairs.

Name: _____ Date: _____

Theodore Roosevelt Becomes President: Activity

Directions: Use information from the reading selection to explain the terms below.

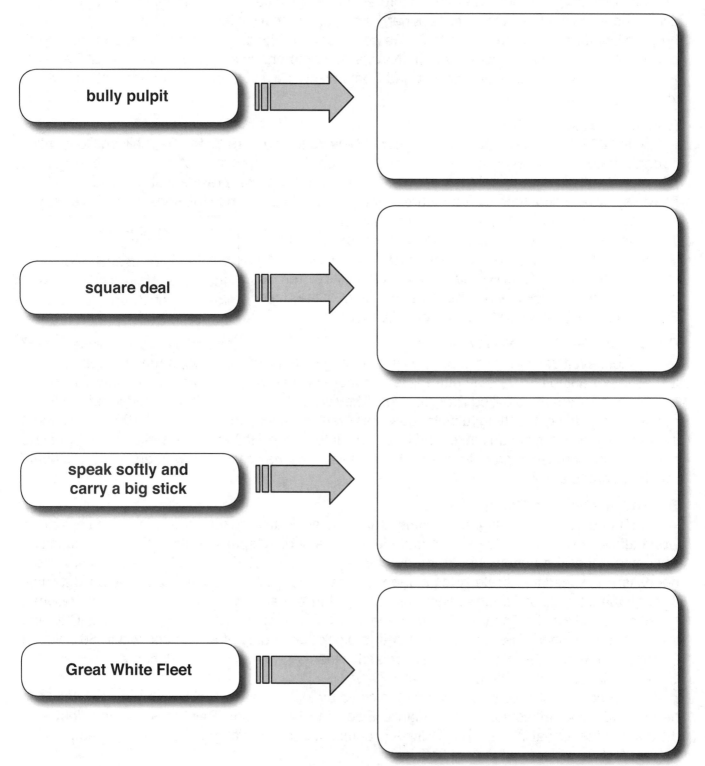

Explanation

bully pulpit

square deal

speak softly and carry a big stick

Great White Fleet

President William Howard Taft

As the election of 1908 neared, Theodore Roosevelt faced the prospect of retirement; the idea did not appeal to him. In looking for a successor, he looked to his old friend William Howard Taft. Taft graduated from Yale University in 1878. He had been a judge in Ohio before McKinley made him solicitor-general (the person who represents the United States before the Supreme Court) and then named him to the Philippines Commission. When Roosevelt became president, he made Taft governor of the Philippines, then Secretary of War. When Roosevelt asked him to run for president in 1908, Taft was nominated and easily defeated William Jennings Bryan and the Democrats in November.

William Howard Taft

Payne-Aldrich Tariff Act

Roosevelt decided this was a good time to take off on an African safari. Taft sent him a warm letter and an expanding ruler so he could measure the animals he killed. Taft began to get himself into trouble. He angered high-tariff Republicans when he asked for a lower tariff. The Payne Bill was passed by the House and lowered the tariff, but Nelson Aldrich's Senate committee amended it 847 times and actually raised the tariff. Taft called the Payne-Aldrich Tariff Act the "best bill the Republican Party ever passed." He also made conservationists angry when he fired Chief Forester Gifford Pinchot, a close friend of Theodore Roosevelt.

Anti-Trust Law

Taft angered some conservatives when he went after the nation's largest corporations for violating the anti-trust law: the American Tobacco Company, Standard Oil, and U.S. Steel. The U.S. Steel case was especially important, since this corporation was accused of breaking the law by buying Tennessee Coal and Iron, a purchase made with Roosevelt's approval. Thus, Taft angered almost every important segment of the Republican Party. When Taft was unhappy, he ate, and his waistline grew to 54 inches.

Woodrow Wilson Becomes President

When Theodore Roosevelt returned from his safari and a much-publicized trip to Europe, many Republicans, including Gifford Pinchot, were at the dock to greet him. At first, Roosevelt said he would stay out of politics; but by 1912, he was often criticizing Taft. Roosevelt clearly wanted another term in the White House. Taft was equally determined to get the Republican

> **Did You Know?**
>
> Taft is the only person to have served as both the president and the chief justice of the Supreme Court.

nomination, and while Roosevelt carried nine states with primaries and Taft carried only one, Roosevelt did not have enough delegates to get the Republican nomination.

Unhappy with Taft being selected, the Roosevelt delegates met two months later in the "Bull Moose" Convention and selected Roosevelt as the candidate for the newly formed Progressive Party. By splitting the Republican Party, they opened the door for the Democratic candidate, Woodrow Wilson, to win the presidency.

In November 1912, Wilson was elected president with less than 42 percent of the popular vote, and Taft came in third with 23.2 percent of the votes. Taft would later be appointed chief justice of the Supreme Court by President Harding in 1921.

Name: _____   Date: _____

President William Howard Taft: Activity

Directions: Use information from the reading selection to complete the page.

1. Place a check mark next to the text features used in the selection.

   ○ title
   ○ headings
   ○ subheadings
   ○ italicized print
   ○ boldface print
   ○ bullets
   ○ photograph
   ○ illustration
   ○ diagram
   ○ chart
   ○ map
   ○ sidebar
   ○ caption

2. Place a check mark next to the organizational structure used in the selection.

   ○ argument/support
   ○ cause/effect
   ○ chronological/sequential
   ○ classification
   ○ compare/contrast
   ○ definition
   ○ description

3. Place a check mark next to the author's purpose for writing the selection.

   ○ to inform
   ○ to entertain
   ○ to persuade

4. List one opinion stated in the reading selection.

   _____

   _____

5. List three important facts you learned.

   A. _____

   B. _____

   C. _____

President Woodrow Wilson

Woodrow Wilson

Woodrow Wilson was the son of a minister. Even though he was dyslexic, he went on to get a bachelor's degree from Princeton, a law degree from the University of Virginia, and a doctor's degree in political science from Johns Hopkins. After years of teaching government at Princeton, he became its president. In 1910, he was elected governor of New Jersey and became the President of the United States in 1913.

Domestic Policy

During his campaign, Wilson promised change. After the election, he was able to put into action the reforms he had promised in his campaign speeches, which became known as the "New Freedom" policy. The policy favored laws that limited big business and helped the small competitor and worker. Some of these laws were the Underwood Tariff Act (lowered tariffs), the Federal Reserve Act (affected banking), and the Clayton Anti-Trust Act (regulated big business).

Relations Between Mexico and the United States

At first, foreign policy was not a big issue, but relations with Mexico became a serious problem. In 1913, President Madero of Mexico was shot by the military leader, General Huerta, who then assumed the presidency. President Wilson recalled the American ambassador and refused to have diplomatic relations with Huerta. When Governor Carranza of Coahuila emerged to challenge Huerta, the United States supported him, and in 1915, Carranza became Mexico's president. Another revolutionary, Poncho Villa, deliberately stirred up trouble between Mexico and the United States, including a raid on Columbus, New Mexico, in March 1916, in which he killed 17 Americans. Wilson sent a force into Mexico under General John J. Pershing, but they never caught Villa.

Interest Turns to World War I

In 1917, Americans were paying closer attention to World War I than to Mexico. War had been going on in Europe since 1914, and it involved the Central Powers (Germany, Austria-Hungary, Bulgaria, and Turkey) on one side and the Allies (England, France, and Russia) on the other side. When the war broke out, Wilson asked Americans to be neutral in thought and in deeds. That was asking the impossible, since one-third of Americans were foreign born or the children of immigrants.

The war in Europe had turned into a stalemate by 1915. Trenches were dug across northern France, and neither side could gain victory on the battlefield. Each side turned to brutal devices to win the war. The Germans began using deadly mustard gas. Using a naval blockade, the British cut off German trade with neutral countries. The Germans countered by using submarines to cut supply lines to England. The airplane, machine gun, and tank made their debuts as weapons.

The United States Enters the War

The German submarine blockade endangered Americans sailing on passenger liners, but Wilson insisted that this was their right, and the Germans must not attack these ships. In 1915, the *Lusitania,* a British ship with 128 Americans on board, was sunk. The American protest was so strong that, for a time, the Germans did not attack. In 1917, the Germans in desperation returned to submarine warfare. The United States declared war, which bothered Wilson's conscience. He said our purpose was "to make the world safe for democracy."

Name: _____ Date: _____

President Woodrow Wilson: Activity

Directions: Use information from the reading selection to answer the questions.

1. What was the impact of Wilson's "New Freedom" policy?

2. Which nations were members of the Central Powers during World War I?

3. Which nations were members of the Allied Powers during World War I?

4. What was the result of the sinking of the *Lusitania*?

The United States Enters World War I

Enthusiasm for the United States entering World War I was not universal. Some men enlisted in the army, but not enough. Some were willing to sacrifice so victory could be won, but not enough. Like a balky mule, the nation had to be harnessed and pointed in the right direction. The usual American freedoms were limited by the need for a common effort, and anyone suspected of disloyalty was sure to suffer for it. New government agencies were created. People and the economy came under new government controls.

U.S. Soldiers in WWI were called Doughboys

The Draft Was Instituted

An army had to be raised, and two million men joined. That was not enough, so the draft was used for the first time since the Civil War. Men from ages 21 to 30 registered for the draft, but a wider age range of 18 to 45 came later. About 2.8 million men were drafted. Of the doughboys (as U.S. soldiers were called in the war), about 2 million went to France, and 1.7 million went into combat. Quick training was provided for new officers, and they became second lieutenants 90 days after entering the army. Sixteen camps were quickly built to house the men. Each camp had 1,200 buildings and was supplied with lights, sewers, and water lines. In 16 other camps, men were housed in tents.

New Agencies Created to Support the War Effort

To support the war effort, many new agencies were created, but only a few of the major ones are included here. Herbert Hoover was appointed head of the Food Administration. Although he was given broad powers, he preferred persuasion. He encouraged people to plant "liberty gardens," so crops raised by farmers could feed allied civilians and armies. Fuel Administrator Harry Garfield persuaded people to turn off their heat on special days, and people sat at home shivering. Former president William Howard Taft chaired the War Labor Board and, with the help of AFL President Samuel Gompers, avoided at least 138 major strikes. The War Industries Board, chaired by Bernard Baruch, controlled raw materials. One important thing this board did was standardize sizes, so instead of having 287 different sizes and types of automobile tires, the number was only 9.

Paying for the War

To pay for the war, the income tax was raised to 4 percent on incomes over $1,000. More money came from "Liberty Loan" drives, and people bought "Liberty Bonds" not only as an investment but to show loyalty. About $21.5 billion was raised in loans, and $11.3 billion was raised in taxes.

Building Patriotic Spirit

To build patriotic spirit, the Creel Committee (Committee on Public Information) was created. It put out millions of pamphlets and books and recruited volunteer speakers to drum up support. Some people refused to back the war. The Sedition Act punished anyone trying to slow the sale of Liberty Bonds or speak against the government. Eugene Debs, the Socialist Party leader, was sentenced to ten years in prison for attacking capitalism. He was released in 1921. Anything German was unpopular. Some people with German names changed them to English names. Dachshunds became "liberty dogs," and German measles became "liberty measles."

Name: _____ Date: _____

The United States Enters World War I: Activity

Directions: Use the information from the reading selection to answer the question.

How did the United States solve the problems created by its entry into World War I?

▼

Problem: Need for Soldiers **Solution:**	**Problem:** Gaining Support for the War Effort **Solution:**
Problem: Paying for the War **Solution:**	**Problem:** Building Patriotic Spirit **Solution:**

Doughboys Are Sent to France

On August 4, 1914, Germany invaded Belgium, starting World War I. Each country's allies joined in the war. Europe was split into two groups: the Allied Powers and the Central Powers. The main members of the Allied Powers were France, Russia, Britain, and later the United States. The main members of the Central Powers were Germany, Austria-Hungary, Bulgaria, and Turkey.

In 1917, Czar Nicholas II was overthrown in Russia, and after a brief try at democracy, the Bolsheviks (communists) took over. In 1918, led by Lenin, Russia dropped out of the war and signed a peace treaty giving up much territory in Eastern Europe. Germany could now throw the weight of its army against the Western Front.

English and French army morale was very low, and when French generals ordered their troops "over the top" (an advance on German trenches), the soldiers refused. The sooner American troops joined the war effort, the better the chances the Allies would survive.

America Prepares for War

The Americans had many things to do before they could aid the Allies. For a nation of its size and importance, the United States had one of the smallest standing armies in the world. Normally less than 200,000, it suddenly jumped to 640,000 in 1917 and over 2.8 million in 1918. Not only did this bring enormous problems in supplying the troops but also in preparing these civilians to fight a highly trained and much-experienced foe. Farmers, mechanics, and shopkeepers had to learn to obey orders, salute, march, fire weapons, and use gas masks. In some camps, soldiers drilled with broomsticks rather than rifles, and barrels hung between poles were used to imitate horseback riding for cavalry recruits. General John J. Pershing was a stickler for military precision and wanted his men to look like an army when they arrived in France.

In the meantime, the Navy had to break the submarine menace that was destroying transport ships faster than they could be replaced. Admiral William Sims decided to use a convoy system to get the ships through. Each group of transport ships would be protected by destroyer escorts all the way across the ocean.

In France, Pershing gathered the supplies of food and forage that his men and draft animals would need. He also had to buy cannons, airplanes, and even uniform buttons because the United States did not produce enough.

American Troops Take Part in War

In July of 1917, the first U.S. troops (doughboys) arrived in France. After more training in trench warfare and gas-mask drills, they were sent to the front. The three most important battles in which Americans took part were at Chateau-Thierry, Belleau Wood, and the Meuse-Argonne campaign. Some Americans distinguished themselves. Private Alvin York, a pacifist turned soldier, went out on patrol, killed at least 15 Germans, and returned with 132 prisoners. He was promoted to sergeant. In the air war, Eddie Rickenbacker became America's flying ace, shooting down 26 German planes.

In 1918, the war was not going well for Germany. The exhausted German Army was running low on food and fuel. When it became apparent they were going to lose the war, Kaiser Wilhelm II gave up his throne. Two days later, the Germans signed the armistice on November 11, 1918, ending the war.

The United States suffered 50,900 deaths (48,000 in combat and 2,900 missing in action). In comparison, England lost 947,000, and France lost 1.38 million. But whether or not the world was safer for democracy was the great unanswered question of the moment.

Name: _____ Date: _____

Doughboys Are Sent to France: Activity

Directions: Use information from the reading selection to complete the activities below.

World War I				
Who were the Allied Powers and Central Powers?	What happened?	Where did it happen?	When did it happen?	Why did it happen?

Three new words I learned: (If you need help use an online or print dictionary.)		
Word: Definition:	Word: Definition:	Word: Definition:

One opinion stated in the reading selection:	Three important facts I learned:

Wilson Goes to Versailles

Woodrow Wilson

Wilson Calls for the Nation to Pull Together

President Woodrow Wilson did not enter World War I lightly. He believed that if we were to go to war, it would have to be for some worthy reason, or the lives of the dead would be lost in vain. He said, "The world must be made safe for democracy. Its peace must be planted upon the tested foundations of political liberty. We have no selfish end to serve."

During the war, Wilson asked that the usual political debate be set aside and that the nation pull together. Many observed this truce, but some were too angry with Wilson to keep silent. One was Theodore Roosevelt, who wanted to organize a new Rough Rider unit to go to France. Wilson turned him down, and Roosevelt became bitter. Many Americans of German and Austrian heritage were anti-Wilson. The Irish hated England for refusing to give Ireland its independence, so they opposed helping England. Socialists saw World War I as a war to save capitalism, not democracy. Eugene Debs, the Socialist Party leader, said, "The master class has always declared the war, and the subject class has always fought the battles." Clearly, Debs did not have the same vision of the purpose of the war that Wilson had.

Fourteen Points for Lasting Peace

On January 8, 1918, President Wilson gave his "Speech of the Fourteen Points." The speech outlined his plan for lasting peace and the end of World War I. His plan included open diplomacy, freedom of the seas, arms reductions, removal of economic barriers, the return of Alsace-Lorraine to France (Germany had seized the region in 1871), an independent Poland, and freedom for minorities in Austria-Hungary and Turkey. The 14th point was most important to him: "A general association of nations" to protect the "political independence of great and small states alike." Many people around the world cheered Wilson's name after they read copies of the Fourteen Points in their own languages.

Election of 1918

In 1918, while war continued, the United States held its off-year elections for the House and Senate. On October 25, two weeks before the election, Wilson appealed to the voters: "If you have approved of my leadership…I earnestly beg that you will express yourselves…by returning a Democratic majority to both the Senate and the House of Representatives." When the election results came in, the Republicans had won control of both the House and Senate.

Wilson Goes to Versailles with His Fourteen-Points Plan

After the election, Wilson announced that he would lead the American peace delegation to the peace conference at Versailles. There were reasons for him to go. The United States had furnished financial backing and troops for the war and should be highly visible at the conference. He could not trust Premier Clemenceau of France or Prime Minister David Lloyd George of England to push the ideals of the Fourteen Points.

But there were reasons for him *not* to go. He had never dealt with foreign leaders person to person; many feared he could not hold his own. There were pressing problems at home to be solved. When he chose to take no leading Republicans or any senators, he would face a hostile crowd when he returned with his treaty.

Name: _____ Date: _____

Wilson Goes to Versailles: Activity

Directions: Answer each question using information from the reading selection.

Question	Answer
1. Why was Theodore Roosevelt angry with Wilson?	
2. Why did the Irish-Americans oppose the war?	
3. Why did the Socialists oppose the United States entering the war?	
4. What was President Wilson's plan for ending the war and obtaining lasting peace?	

The Treaty of Versailles and the League of Nations

On November 11, 1918, an armistice was declared, ending World War I. In 1919, President Woodrow Wilson went to Versailles for peace negotiations. He wanted to do more than just solve the issues left from World War I; he dreamed of ending all wars forever. In Europe, he was greeted by huge crowds. American newspapers sent their best writers to cover the conference. As delegates from thirty countries gathered in the city to draw up the Treaty of Versailles, laying out peace terms, it appeared there would be plenty of news for them to cover.

The Paris Peace Conference

Thirty was too large a number for negotiating, so it was reduced to the Council of Ten, then the Council of Four (U.S., England, France, Italy), and then the Council of Three (U.S., England, France). The doors were closed, and reporters got only brief statements of what was going on inside. Italy's Orlando wanted to take land from Austria, England's Lloyd George wanted German colonies, and France's Clemenceau wanted to cripple Germany so badly she would not be able to fight again for many years. Wilson, the American idealist, wanted to make the world "safe for democracy." He urged the leaders to accept his idea for a League of Nations and make it part of the Treaty of Versailles.

Lloyd George and Clemenceau were lukewarm on the League of Nations idea, but Wilson regarded the League as the most critical part of their work. Despite their opinion to the contrary, he would not allow it to be separated from the rest of the treaty. When he returned home, he tried to convince the Senate that the League was essential, but many did not like what they saw. Senator Henry Cabot Lodge wrote the Round Robin resolution, which said that the League in its existing form was unacceptable.

When Wilson returned to France, he found that Clemenceau wanted changes made in the treaty. He wanted Germany to pay for pensions for French soldiers, and he wanted to take German territory to the Rhine River. Both Wilson's battles with Clemenceau and the flu were draining to his health. He had to give in to Italian demands for the port city of Fiume (at the northern tip of the Adriatic Sea) and to Japanese demands for Shantung. In June of 1919, Germany signed the Versailles Treaty agreeing it: (1) would be disarmed, (2) had to sign a blank check for French pensions, and (3) had to take all the blame for creating the war. They protested, but they had no choice except to sign.

United States Rejects Treaty of Versailles and League of Nations

Wilson returned home and placed his treaty before the Senate. Instead of acting quickly, the Senate referred it to the Foreign Relations Committee, chaired by Wilson's enemy, Senator Lodge. The Senate was divided by three opinions. *Internationalists* wanted the treaty to be accepted without changes. *Reservationists* were willing to accept the treaty, but with major changes. *Irreconcilables* opposed the League of Nations in any form.

Wilson took his League to the American people and went on a nationwide speaking tour. His health worsened, and he rushed back to Washington, D.C., where he suffered a paralytic stroke. He refused to give in to suggested changes in the treaty. Without compromise, the Senate rejected the treaty. Wilson wanted the League of Nations to be the big campaign issue of 1920, but the public had tired of the subject, and Warren Harding, a Republican, was elected president by a vote of 16 million to 9 million.

Name: _____ Date: _____

The Treaty of Versailles and the League of Nations: Activity

Directions: Complete the graphic organizer for the terms listed below. Write a definition for each word and use it in a sentence. Use an online or print dictionary if you need help.

armistice	Definition
	Sentence

treaty	Definition
	Sentence

delegate	Definition
	Sentence

league	Definition
	Sentence

President Harding's Reputation Is Hurt by Scandals

Warren Harding

By 1920, the nation was tired of idealism. Progressives had wanted to end big business control of the economy, but the rich were as powerful as ever. Overseas, the war to make the world "safe for democracy" had only added new colonies to England and France, feeble governments in central Europe, and communist rule in Russia. People wanted a different kind of leader than President Woodrow Wilson, and they found it in Warren Harding. A small-town editor from Ohio, he had been helped up the political ladder by his friend Harry Daugherty and his wife. He had served as a state senator, lieutenant governor, and U.S. senator. After other presidential hopefuls had been cancelled out, Republican Party leaders picked Harding because he was not controversial.

Harding Elected President

Warren Harding was elected president in 1920. His impressive appearance, outgoing personality, and the ability to dodge controversial issues helped him win the presidency. His Cabinet was a mixture of capable leaders and poor choices. Among the capable were Andrew Mellon (Treasury), Herbert Hoover (Commerce), and Charles Evans Hughes (State). But there were old friends from back home (the "Ohio Gang" as they came to be called) and Washington friends, and they were the ones who brought him down. Harry Daugherty became attorney general, and Senator Albert Fall (New Mexico) became secretary of the interior. Charles Forbes became director of the Veterans Administration. His military career included both desertion and being a Congressional Medal of Honor recipient.

Scandals in the Harding Administration

Harding did not interfere with his able Cabinet members, and they made some important changes. Mellon discovered that the United States had never had a budget, and a Budgeting Act was passed. Hughes pushed for navy limitations, and the Washington Naval Conference was held, which reduced the number of battleships and heavy cruisers. With both inflation and unemployment very low, it appeared that the nation was in good hands.

There were some disturbing signs, though. The president's statements to the press indicated that he did not understand many important issues. Then some government officials committed suicide. Government oil reserves at Teapot Dome, Wyoming, and Elk Hills, California, were leased to oil men by the Interior Department without any bidding. Secretary Fall was able to fix up his New Mexico ranch, which had always lost money, and to pay off all back taxes; his salary was $10,000 a year. Rumors spread about a "little house on K Street" where bribes were offered to officials as they drank liquor seized by prohibition agents. President Harding's health began to break, and his doctor ordered him to take a trip to the West Coast. While still in office, he died of an apparent heart attack in 1923; Calvin Coolidge then became president.

The nation mourned a fallen leader but soon began to scorn him as one instance after another of misconduct in his administration was revealed. Forbes and his friends stole millions of dollars from the Veterans Administration; Forbes went to prison. The Teapot Dome scandal exposed Secretary Fall as the receiver of bribes from oil men; he was sent to prison and fined. Daugherty was nearly convicted of receiving bribes and was forced to resign in 1924. All of these people are now only a faint memory, but Harding's reputation was ruined forever.

Name: _____ Date: _____

President Harding's Reputation Is hurt by Scandals: Activity

A **political cartoon** is a cartoon or comic strip created to communicate a social or political message. It is a way for cartoonists to express an opinion about a topic.

Directions: Go online to the URL <https://www.britannica.com/event/Teapot-Dome-Scandal>. Examine the cartoon. Use your observations to complete the chart.

List people, objects, and activities in the photograph.		
People	Objects	Activities

List words or phrases found in the cartoon.

Based on the reading selection and your observations, what can you infer about the message of the political cartoon?

The Automobile Changes American Life

Although the automobile could trace its ancestry to China, France, England, and Germany, it was American producers like Ransom Olds, William Durant, and Henry Ford who made it the commonplace product that transformed twentieth-century life. At first, it was seen as a nuisance and a rich man's toy; but when the car came into the price range of the average person, everyone wanted one. A woman in the 1920s was asked why she owned a car but did not have a bathtub. She answered, "You can't go to town in a bathtub." The United States was a nation on the go, and it wanted to get there in its own car.

Henry Ford

Early History of the Automobile

Early efforts centered on steam and electric cars, but the steamer was too slow and complicated, and the electric was too limited in distance. The Stanley Steamer did have some success, but it was too expensive for most people. The internal combustion engine created power more quickly and had a longer range than steam and electric cars. The first American car company was owned by the Duryea brothers, and their automobile won the car race from Chicago to Evanston, Illinois, in 1895.

Improvements to the Automobile

An important step in car building came with interchangeable parts. This began in 1901 when a fire occurred at the factory of Ransom Olds, who produced little runabouts. To continue production, he ordered parts from other companies and specified the sizes and shapes he needed. This idea expanded when Henry Leland's Cadillac Company developed standardized parts for all its cars. Other changes made cars more functional. Electric headlights replaced earlier gaslights, the self-starter prevented arm injuries, and enclosed cars made traveling more comfortable in cold weather.

Henry Ford

Henry Ford made the car more affordable. He organized the Ford Motor Company in 1903, and five years later came out with his first Model T. The price of $850 was too high for the average person, so he found ways to cut costs. One method was the assembly line, where parts came by conveyor belts to the point where they were added to the frame. Other ways in which he reduced costs were to paint all cars black and to make his own parts. By 1925, a new Model T sold for only $260.

But Ford was losing out against General Motors. Formed in 1908 by William C. Durant, GM bought up Buick and Oldsmobile in 1908, Oakland and Cadillac in 1909, and the moderately priced Chevrolet line in 1911. GM boasted that it had a car "within the price range of all."

Other small companies were also in business, and some, like Packard, Nash, and Hudson, survived for many years. Walter Chrysler, who had been president of Buick, started Chrysler Corporation in 1925, and with his Chryslers, Dodges, and Plymouths became the third of the "Big Three."

Americans purchased cars at record rates. In 1904, 54,000 U.S. cars were registered; in 1914, there were 1.6 million on American roads; and ten years later, 15.4 million. With so many people owning cars, there were demands for better roads, roadside hotels, tourist attractions, gasoline stations, and repair garages. The car changed society. Rural areas were no longer as isolated, suburbs grew, and Americans traveled farther.

Name: _____ Date: _____

The Automobile Changes American Life: Activity

Directions: Answer the following questions. Support your answers with information from the reading selection.

1. What was the problem with early steam and electric cars?

2. What improvements made the automobile more functional?

3. How was Ford able to lower the cost of the Model T from $850 to $260?

4. How did the automobile change society?

The Stock Market Collapses

If individuals want to know whether they are getting ahead financially, they count the money in their pockets and in their bank accounts. But if one wants to know how the nation is doing, he looks at the stock market as an indicator to whether investors feel confident or gloomy about the future. When the market keeps going up, it is said to be a "bull" market, but when it continues to drop, it is a "bear" market. Sometimes, there is a *correction*, meaning that prices are a little too high, so it takes a short drop.

The Stock Market in the 1920s

In the 1920s, many people invested in the market, believing it would always go up. Stockbrokers (those who handle the sale of stocks) encouraged investment by selling stocks "on margin." A person could buy a stock by paying only 10 percent of its value. A $10 stock could be bought for $1. The broker put up the other $9, but if the price dropped to say $8, the buyer would have to put up the extra $1 or the broker would sell the stock, and the buyer would lose his investment. As long as the prices of stock on the New York Stock Exchange were going up, people gave little thought to the risks.

Warning Signs of a Collapse

Investors paid no attention to many warning signs that prosperity was fragile. The sorry state of the farm economy was one sign; many farmers could not make it and left their farms to take jobs in town. They were not buying farm equipment, which slowed down the farm implement business. Also, some Americans invested in the Florida land boom of the mid-1920s in the hope of making a fortune when someone wanted to buy the land from them at a fabulous profit. This was called the "Florida Bubble." However, in 1926 two hurricanes that hit Florida caused people to decide to invest elsewhere, and those who owned land there had to dump it for whatever price they could get. Those who had lost money were less inclined to gamble after that. Many Americans were too poor to buy radios, washing machines, and new cars; they did not add to the economy. Many people in the market thought it was too high, and they took their money out. With fewer people to buy stock, the market began to drop. Finally, big banks made many bad loans to nations with weak economies. That left them with little reserve when those countries defaulted (could not pay their debts).

Stock Market Collapses

The first signs of trouble came in September 1929, when the market dipped; but after it came up for a time, investors assumed it was just a correction. On October 23, major stocks dropped rapidly, but banks bought up stocks to keep a panic from occurring. On October 29, 1929, panic hit the market. Everyone wanted to sell stocks, and no one wanted to buy. Brokers called investors and told them to "put up more margin," but they could not begin to cover the losses, and more stocks were put up for sale.

> **Quick Fact**
>
> The stock market lost $14 billion on October 29, 1929. This day is known as "Black Tuesday."

The market steadied after that because no one could believe that the bull market was dead. From September 3 to the end of October, stock prices dropped: AT&T dropped $106 a share, General Electric by $228.13 a share, and RCA from $101 to $28 a share. Some companies could hardly sell their stock for any price. Many investors lost everything, including their money, their dreams, and their confidence.

Name: _____   Date: _____

The Stock Market Collapses: Activity

Directions: From the reading selection, select four warning signs of the stock market collapse of 1929 and its effect on the economy.

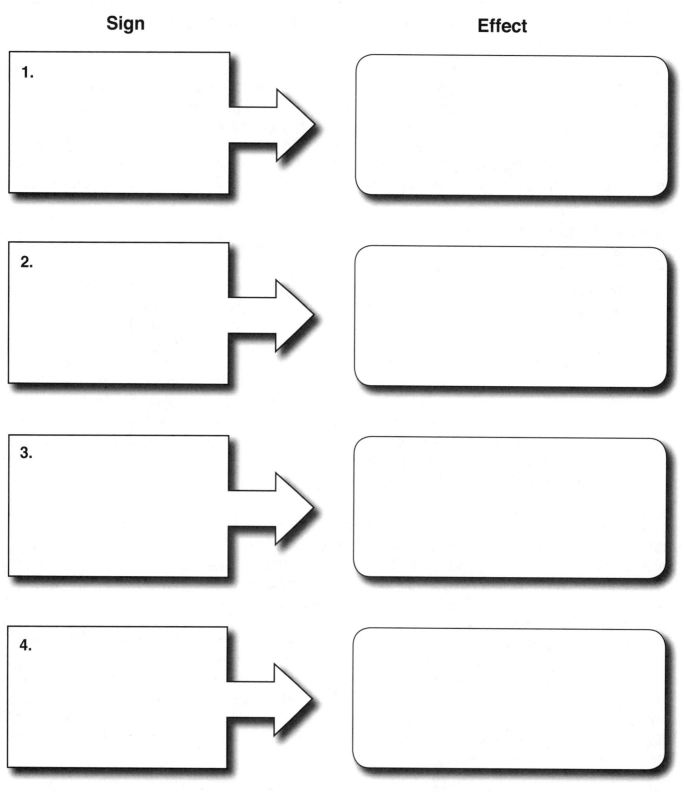

Sign

Effect

1.

2.

3.

4.

Herbert Hoover and the Great Depression

As Herbert Hoover looked out the White House windows, he felt like the coach of a losing team. No matter what he tried, nothing seemed to work. Like almost everyone else, he felt that the stock market drop was only temporary, and soon the economy would get back to normal. As a good and decent man who believed that if people cooperated anything could be solved, he relied on the method that had always served him well—he called meetings. Governors and business executives were asked to start new spending programs and avoid the temptation of cutting wages; they agreed. Labor unions were asked not to threaten strikes that would hamper recovery, and they agreed. That policy usually would have ended the problem; but this time, there was a gloom that took confidence and hope away. People did not worry about getting ahead; they were only concerned with surviving.

When consumers stopped buying, producers started laying off workers. Banks stopped lending money because they feared their depositors would all want to take their deposits from the bank at the same time (a run), and they did not have the cash on hand for such an event. Banks began to pressure borrowers to pay off their loans, and they tightened credit. Stores tried using sales to attract customers, but with no money, they could not afford even a good bargain.

Agricultural Marketing Act of 1929

Farmers, who did not enjoy prosperity in the 1920s, faced a drop in the prices of farm goods in the grocery store. When the cost of buying seed, equipment, and rail transportation became higher than the price they could sell food for in the city, farmers stopped shipping their crops and found ways to use them to feed their families. Milk needed by children in town was dumped into the gully. To help the farmer, Hoover and Congress created the Agricultural Marketing Act in 1929. The government bought up $500 million worth of farm products and asked farmers to cut back production. Farmers, desperate to meet their mortgage payments, raised more; so the farm problem continued. The Midwest and Southern Plains regions experienced a severe drought in 1931. In 1932, dust storms spread across the Midwest, earning the region the name "the dust bowl." The number of storms doubled the following year. In 1934, the United States experienced one of its worst droughts ever, affecting the Central and Western states.

Reconstruction Finance Corporation (RFC)

To encourage economic activity, the Reconstruction Finance Corporation was established by Congress on January 22, 1932. That year, the RFC loaned $1.5 billion to railroads, banks, and corporations. That effort did not work either, as those companies used it to pay debts or dividends.

> **Quick Fact**
>
> From 1932 to 1957, the RFC distributed over 40 billion in loans and investments.

Unemployment Continues to Rise

Unemployment increased from 3 million in 1929 to 9 million in 1931 and to 13 million in 1932. This meant that one out of every four Americans was unemployed, and many who had jobs worked only part of the day or two or three days a week. Employers were cutting wages, in many cases just to keep the company from going under. Millions of Americans were unemployed, hungry, and without housing for the first time in U.S. history. As desperate as the situation was, only a few thousand Americans turned to communism or socialism as the answer. But in 1932, they threw Hoover and his party out of office by an electoral vote of 472–59.

Name: _____ Date: _____

Herbert Hoover and the Great Depression: Activity

Directions: Examine the map below; then answer the questions.

Percentage of State Population Receiving Unemployment Relief, 1934

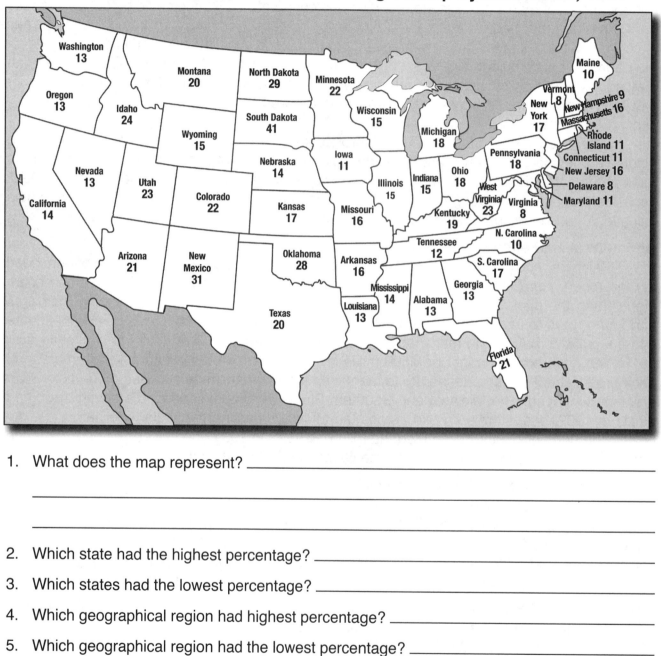

1. What does the map represent? _____

   _____

   _____

2. Which state had the highest percentage? _____

3. Which states had the lowest percentage? _____

4. Which geographical region had highest percentage? _____

5. Which geographical region had the lowest percentage? _____

6. How does the map contribute to your understanding of the reading selection?

   _____

   _____

Roosevelt and the New Deal

FDR and the New Deal

With unemployment nearly 25 percent, 5,500 banks closed, farmers threatened with losing their land, soup kitchens in cities, and many factories closed, millions of Americans anxiously waited to see what President-elect Franklin D. Roosevelt (usually referred to as FDR) would do. When he accepted the Democratic nomination, he had pledged himself to a "New Deal" for the American people. Now the nation wanted to know what kind of new deal he would give them.

FDR's Inaugural Address

In his inaugural address on March 4, 1933, FDR expressed confidence that "this great Nation will endure as it has endured," and "the only thing we have to fear is fear itself." He asked for emergency powers to defeat the Depression, just as if it were an enemy country that had invaded the United States. With a Cabinet consisting of Democrats, two Republicans, and one woman (Frances Perkins), he acted swiftly to solve different problems. His first move was to close all banks until their records could be examined, and then the weak banks were closed permanently. He hoped this would restore public confidence in banks. He used his first "fireside chat" radio address to assure the people their money would be safe when the banks reopened. It worked, and when banks opened, people walked in to deposit and not to withdraw money.

> ### Quick Fact
> Roosevelt signed the Social Security Act into law on August 14, 1935.

Relief Aid and Job Creation

During his first 104 days in office, FDR asked Congress for 15 pieces of legislation and got all of them. These created many new agencies, usually known by their alphabet names.

The Agricultural Adjustment Act (AAA) went to work on the farm problem. Under Henry Wallace, it paid farmers to take land out of production. Since the 1933 crop was already in the ground, it had to be destroyed. To raise pork prices, thousands of pigs were killed; their bodies were ground up and buried. For city dwellers, all of this meant higher prices at a time when they could not afford it. But other New Deal programs were also at work.

To help states with relief projects, the Federal Emergency Relief Act (FERA) gave grants of $500 million, but the idea of giving people money they hadn't earned was not nearly as popular as giving them jobs so they could earn the money. The Civilian Conservation Corps (CCC) employed about 300,000 young men; they were paid $30 a month ($25 of that was sent to their families), given room and board, lived in military barracks, and worked at conservation projects. Public Works Administration (PWA) was another program to hire the unemployed, but it moved so slowly that it was replaced by the Civil Works Administration (CWA) in November 1933, and Works Progress Administration (WPA) replaced it in 1935.

The National Recovery Act (NRA) was created to encourage business growth. An industry (like steel or petroleum) was to draw up codes of fair competition, which included how much they would charge. This was to prevent cutthroat competition. Codes also set wages at no less than 30¢ an hour, abolished child labor, and required businesses to deal with labor unions. A business abiding by the code could display a "blue eagle" on its products.

What Were the Results?

The New Deal was a turning point in history, as the government began to regulate and involve itself in the economy. At first, the public was nearly 100 percent behind the changes, but in time, critics raised questions.

Name: _____ Date: _____

Roosevelt and the New Deal: Activity

Directions: Listed in the chart are some of the Congressional Acts passed during Roosevelt's first 100 days in office. Research each act; then write a summary.

Congressional Acts	Summary
1. Emergency Bank Relief Act	
2. Government Economy Act	
3. Federal Emergency Relief Act	
4. Agricultural Adjustment Act	
5. Emergency Farm Mortgage Act	
6. Securities Act of 1933	
7. Homeowner's Loan Act	
8. National Recovery Act	
9. Glass-Steagall Act of 1933	
10. Emergency Railroad Transportation Act	

The World Is Threatened by Dictators

The world envisioned by Woodrow Wilson at Versailles was one that was made safe for democracy. Nations would form governments by fair elections, and the boundaries of all nations would be guaranteed. With no threat of attack, the money always spent in the past on the military could be used for health, education, and economic development. By the 1930s, Wilson's dream seemed gone forever, as desperate nations turned to strong leaders who had no morals and who cared only about their own survival and national glory. The spread of the Depression across the globe added supporters to their causes, even in democratic countries.

Communism in Russia

When Vladimir Lenin's communists came to power in Russia, they threatened world revolution. In 1924, Lenin died, and Josef Stalin took over. As a man who had survived imprisonment and Siberian exile many times, Stalin killed, imprisoned, or exiled anyone who even thought of replacing him or who stood in his way. Communist parties developed in other countries, and anti-communists were terrified that unless they found someone able to keep communists out, they would lose their property and influence.

Fascism in Italy

Italy was a poor country after World War I—especially in the south—and was a good breeding ground for communism. With many parties in Italy, the parliament was so tied up with organizational problems that it could not deal with the growing violence and economic problems of Italy. A group called Fascists were ready to use force to battle communists. In 1922, the king appointed the Fascists' leader, Benito Mussolini, as premier. Within a year, he had all the power of a dictator.

Germany and the Third Reich

Germany was also torn by bitter battles among various groups. The Weimar Republic, as the government formed after World War I was called, had very little public support. When economic troubles came after 1929, the upper and middle classes feared the strong communist movement among the lower class. One of the most radical groups was the Nazi party, led by Adolf Hitler. After he was arrested in 1923, Hitler wrote his ideas out in *Mein Kampf (My Struggle)*, blaming most of Germany's problems on the nation's Jews. In 1933, he became Germany's chancellor, and in 1934, he became chancellor and president. Calling his regime the "Third Reich," he made life miserable for Jews, forcing some of Germany's most brilliant scientists to escape the country. Others were not so lucky and ended up in concentration camps; by 1945, at least 6 million Jews had been killed.

Military Rule in Japan

Japan faced a serious population problem in the 1920s that threatened the fragile liberal government of Japan. Low on raw materials, the Japanese used their low-paid workers to compete in the world market. That did well until the Depression cut outside markets. After the liberal prime minister was shot in 1930, the military took over, silenced any opposition in the Diet (parliament), and prepared for a war on China.

What Were the Results?

Merciless rulers were using hard times to take control of their nations. It was only a matter of time before they would threaten their weaker neighbors and bring the world to war.

Name: _____   Date: _____

The World Is Threatened by Dictators: Activity

Directions: Use information from the reading selection to complete the graphic organizer.

Headings   **Key Details**

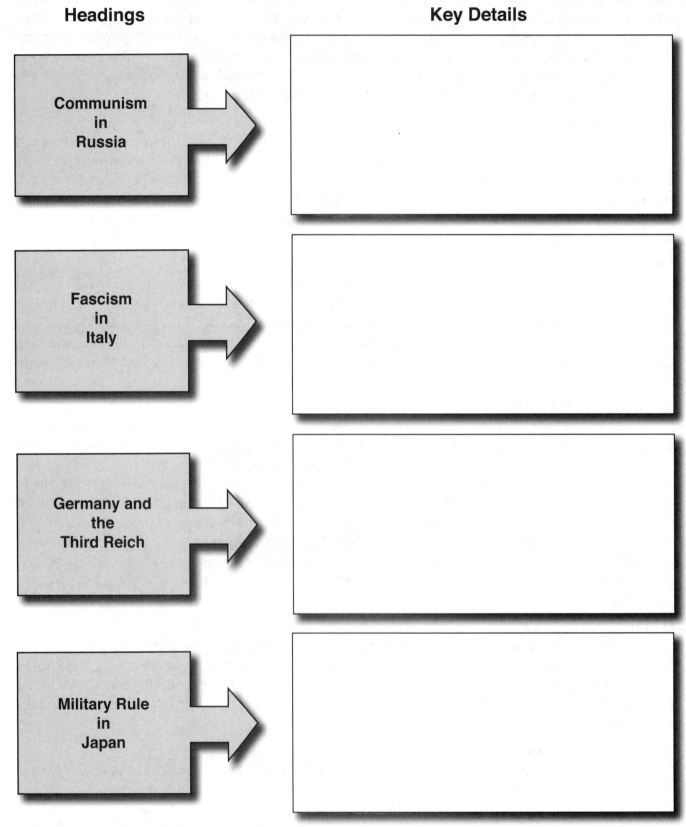

World War II Reaches America

Not content to control their own people, the dictators also wanted to take freedom away from others. Hitler said Germany needed *Lebensraum* (living room); the Russian goal was to "liberate the masses" from their capitalist tyrants; and the Japanese wanted a "new order" in Asia. Using the economic stress and self-concern of democratic nations, they threatened their neighbors and warned them that unless they bowed to superior force, they would face serious consequences.

Expansion by Invasion

In 1931, Japan invaded Manchuria, which belonged to China; after the Chinese boycotted Japanese goods, Shanghai was attacked the next year. No one acted against Japan, and other greedy nations saw opportunities open for expansion. Italy attacked Ethiopia in 1935 with modem weapons, while defenders bravely resisted, using ancient guns and spears. Again, little was done. In 1936, German troops occupied the Rhineland. On November 1, 1936, Mussolini announced that Germany and Italy were forming the Rome-Berlin Axis. Japan would join later that year.

Spanish Fascists, led by Francisco Franco, revolted against the government in 1936, and each side reached out for support. The Spanish Republicans were aided by Russia, and the Fascists were helped by Italy and Germany. The major countries used this war to try new weapons, and they sent "volunteers" to help fight. By 1939, the war was over, with about 750,000 people killed and Franco in full control.

Austria, Germany's southern neighbor, was the next target for expansion, and German troops, with the full support of many Austrians, marched into Vienna. The Sudeten section of Czechoslovakia, with a large number of German-speaking residents, was next. This time, England and France objected, and a conference was held at Munich. Hitler assured the English and French that Germany had no further ambitions to expand. But he did not keep his word, and Germans soon occupied all of Czechoslovakia.

France and England Declare War on Germany

The invasion of Poland by Germany was too much, and England and France declared war on Germany on September 1, 1939. World War II officially began. Within a year, Norway, Holland, Belgium, Luxembourg, and France fell to the Nazis.

Americans listened to radio reports of the fall of Paris, the air war over England, Hitler's attack on Russia, and Japanese attacks on China. The United States was not neutral in thought but did not want to fight. The Nye Committee report in 1935 convinced Americans that World War I had been fought to protect selfish interests of bankers and arms makers. Neutrality laws were passed to avoid repeating the "mistakes" of World War I.

Attack on Pearl Harbor

The America First Committee, made up of many prominent citizens, was alarmed as Roosevelt inched closer toward helping England by sending supplies, trading 50 old destroyers for bases, and escorting convoys to Greenland. However, it was the Japanese who brought the United States into the war by their sneak attack on the U.S. naval base at Pearl Harbor on December 7, 1941. The attack began at approximately 7:55 A.M. and lasted over two hours. When the attack was over, approximately 2,400 servicemen were dead and almost 1,200 were wounded. Of the eight battleships sitting in the harbor, four were sunk. On December 8, President Roosevelt asked Congress for a declaration of war against Japan. In his speech, Roosevelt called December 7, 1941, "a date which will live in infamy." Congress granted the declaration of war.

Name: _____ Date: _____

World War II Reaches America: Activity

Directions: Use information from the reading selection to develop a time line (from earliest to latest date) identifying the events leading up to America's entry into World War II. The first one is done for you.

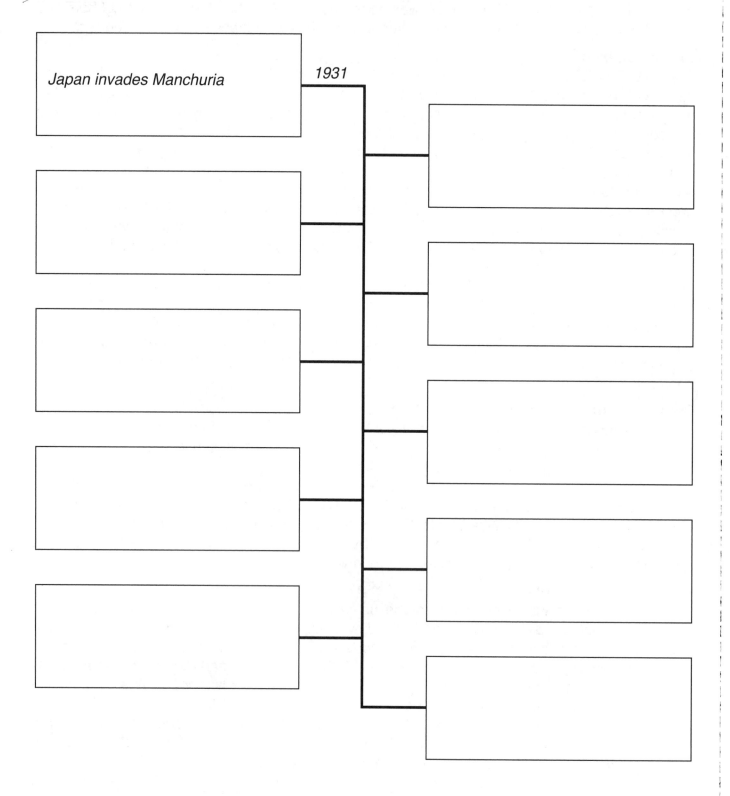

Japan invades Manchuria   1931

The Nation Mobilizes for War

United States Enters World War II

On December 8, 1941, the day after the attack on Pearl Harbor, long lines gathered in front of recruiting stations, and in Washington, President Franklin D. Roosevelt (FDR) gave an eloquent speech to Congress proclaiming December 7 a "date which will live in infamy." By a unanimous vote, the Senate voted for war, and only one House member voted against war. The debate over whether the United States should enter the war was over, and very few Americans did not give it full support.

"Arsenal for Democracy"

The United States had begun gearing up for war with the draft in 1940 and increased military production (to make the United States what Roosevelt called "the arsenal for democracy"). The president set high, and some said impossible, goals for production, and all of them were exceeded. Factories that had been shut down in 1938 went to eight-hour shifts in 1939, and by 1942, they were turning out products 24 hours a day. In 1938, the United States put out 3,800 aircraft per year; by 1940, that was up to 12,804 aircraft. Roosevelt said that the United States must raise that to 50,000 planes a year. In 1942, 47,000 planes were manufactured, and the next year, 85,000 planes came off production lines.

New production techniques were used to build ships. Henry J. Kaiser mass-produced freighters (liberty ships) that could be built by workers in 40 days. By 1945, an aircraft carrier could be built in 16 months, a destroyer in six months.

The War Production Board (WPB) was set up under Donald Nelson to assign where raw materials went, and it coordinated the production of goods needed by the armies and navies, not only of the United States, but of allies as well.

Think About It

Below is a note printed on the back of a ration book used during World War II.

Important: *When you have used your ration, salvage the Tin Cans and Waste Fats. They are needed to make munitions for our fighting men.*

Nearly all civilian production stopped so that factories could devote full attention to military needs. Because scarcity leads to higher prices, the Office of Price Administration (OPA) was created to keep prices in check. Ration books were issued, and when a person bought sugar, gasoline, or any other listed item, they took their billfold and ration book with them. Those with an 'A' sticker on their car were entitled to only four gallons of gasoline a week.

Home Front

With the 450,000-man military force of 1940 increasing to 9 million in 1943, and with factories rushing to fill orders, the unemployment problem of the late 1930s was reversed. Unemployment running at 19 percent in 1938 dropped to only 1.2 percent in 1944. The labor force included many who had always been excluded before. Women held jobs doing nearly every kind of work men had always done; the symbol of the "new woman" was "Rosie the Riveter," with a bandana around her hair and a riveting machine in her hand. Elderly people returned to the workforce in record numbers. African Americans had always found factory jobs closed to them before, but not now; many left the south to find work in the north and west.

A sleeping giant had awakened and supplied not only its own troops and sailors but sent thousands of trucks, tanks, and airplanes to other nations. America had indeed become the "arsenal for democracy," and capitalism proved it could produce better than any other system.

Name: _____ Date: _____

The Nation Mobilizes for War: Activity

Directions: Think about what you have read; then answer the questions below. Cite evidence from the reading selection to support your answers.

1. What effect did the war have on the American labor force?

2. Do you think the author was correct when he states, "America had indeed become the 'arsenal for democracy'"?

General Eisenhower Leads the D-Day Invasion

German military success had swept aside every opposing force by 1941. Moving swiftly against the French, British, and Russians, the German *Wehrmacht* (army) controlled an area from Norway to North Africa and from the tip of France's Normandy peninsula to western Russia. But by 1942, the German advance stalled in Russia and in the deserts of North Africa. British Field Marshall Montgomery's defeat of General Erwin Rommel's *Afrika Korps* stopped the German drive toward the Nile River at El Alamein and offered some relief for the United States and its allies.

Eisenhower Selected for European Command

In Washington, Army Chief of Staff George Marshall was responsible for selecting commanding officers for the various U.S. armies around the globe. Marshall had a keen eye for quality and chose Douglas MacArthur for command in the Pacific. But, he wondered, who should he pick for the European command? The job would require a quick grasp of changing situations, diplomacy in dealing with difficult political and military leaders, and a clear concept of modern war. He passed over many senior officers to choose Dwight Eisenhower. A lieutenant colonel when the war began, Eisenhower had risen very slowly in the peacetime army. While his jobs were routine, they added up to his understanding of many phases of the army. He had trained tank commanders, served in an infantry battalion, had traveled to France twice, and had written a book on French World War I battlefields. He had served on the assistant secretary of war's staff and on MacArthur's staff in the Philippines. He had learned to fly and wore an aviator's wings. Most important was his ability to get along with his peers and to keep the common touch. Often called "Ike," his big smile and outgoing manner gave his men feelings of optimism and trust.

> **Quick Fact**
>
> Eisenhower was promoted to General of the Army (5-stars) on December 20, 1944.

It was this wide knowledge that caused Marshall to pick Eisenhower for command of U.S. troops in Europe. Like Roosevelt, he wanted to attack the French coast first, but Churchill opposed it. When Roosevelt gave in to English pressure, "Operation Torch," the invasion of North Africa, was developed, and Eisenhower was given command. With American troops coming from the west and British troops from the east, the *Afrika Korps* was trapped, and 275,000 German and Italian troops surrendered in May 1943.

The invasion of Sicily began in July 1943; after six weeks, it fell. Then came the landings in Italy, and on June 4, 1944, Rome fell.

"Operation Overlord"

"Operation Overlord," was the code name for the Battle of Normandy (France). This invasion of France was the most extensive, most complex landing operation ever to take place. It involved 3 million men from many nations, 11,000 airplanes, 500 warships, and 4,000 support craft. They were to hit the Germans by surprise. The plan involved tying down German reserve forces so they would not reinforce the troops dug in along the coast. That was accomplished by creating two phony armies to make German generals believe the real landing was a diversion. The plan worked; by the time fresh German troops arrived, the Allies were on the beaches.

What Were the Results?

On June 6, 1944, the D-Day Invasion was the beginning of the end for Hitler. He had some success that winter in the Battle of the Bulge; but after it was stopped, German armies retreated.

Name: _____ Date: _____

General Eisenhower Leads the D-Day Invasion: Activity

Directions: Use information from the reading selection to complete the graphic organizer. Then write a summary.

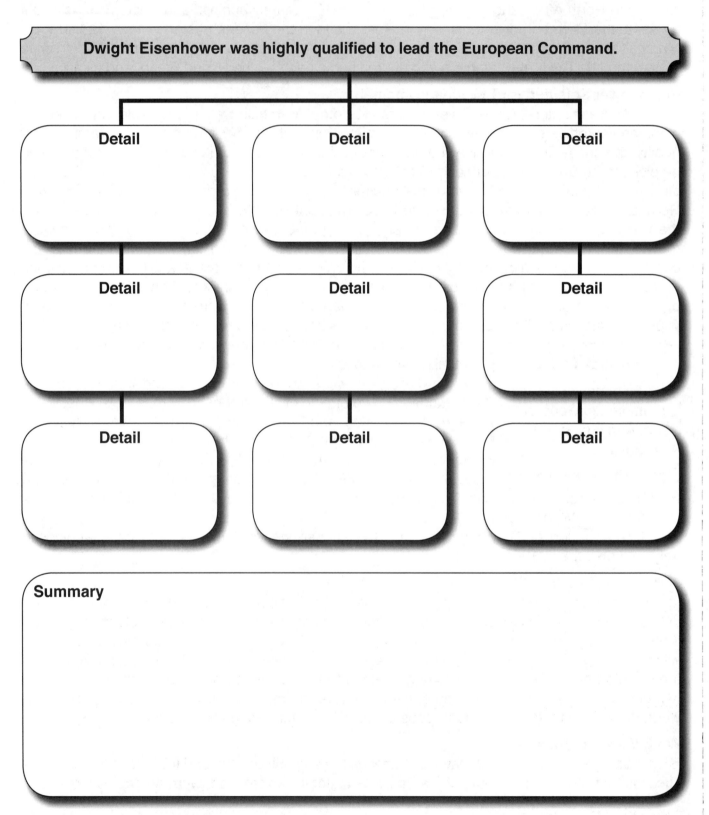

Dwight Eisenhower was highly qualified to lead the European Command.

Detail

Detail

Detail

Detail

Detail

Detail

Detail

Detail

Detail

Summary

Atomic Blasts End World War II

General Douglas MacArthur, commander of U.S. forces in the Pacific, was furious when he learned that President Franklin Roosevelt and General George Marshall considered Germany the enemy that must be defeated first. The humiliating attack on Pearl Harbor and his losses at Bataan and Corregidor in the Philippines made the Japanese his target for retaliation.

Japanese Relocation

Anti-Japanese feeling ran strong on the West Coast of the United States. The Japanese-born non-citizens (Issei) and their American-citizen children (Nisei) were hated by many. Only a few were disloyal, but President Roosevelt gave in to pressure and signed Executive Order 9066, which forbade Japanese to live along the West Coast. Anyone with one-eighth Japanese ancestry was sent to a "relocation camp." Many Nisei joined the army to prove their loyalty.

Battles in the Pacific Theater

For Fleet Admiral Chester Nimitz and MacArthur, the problem was stopping Japan from advancing. Moving quickly at first, the Japanese spread south to New Guinea and the Solomon Islands and north to the islands of Attu and Kiska in the Aleutian chain in the Pacific Ocean. In May 1942, the Battle of the Coral Sea blocked Japan's threat to Australia. Unlike previous naval battles, it was fought entirely with airplanes.

A much more important battle came in June, when a large Japanese fleet sailed toward the small but strategic island of Midway. The island was located 1,135 miles northwest of Honolulu. When Nimitz committed the U.S. fleet to Midway, he took an enormous gamble. Midway cost the Japanese all four of their aircraft carriers engaged in the battle; the United States lost only one.

The marines and army faced the enemy in a long list of battles in the jungles of New Guinea, Guadalcanal, Tarawa, and hundreds of other small islands in the Pacific. The enemy built extensive fortifications and always fought bravely, rarely surrendering. Aid was also sent to China over the very dangerous Ledo Road. In China, Chiang Kai-Shek's Nationalist and Mao Zedong's Communist troops spent more time watching each other than fighting the Japanese, but they provided enough pressure to keep Japanese troops tied down.

In March of 1942, President Roosevelt ordered MacArthur to leave the Philippines in order to avoid capture by the Japanese. MacArthur did not want to leave, but he realized the problem of having a famous American general fall into the hands of the enemy. When he left the Philippines, MacArthur promised, "I shall return." On October 20, 1944, he fulfilled that promise. When a Japanese task force steamed toward the Philippines, Admiral William Halsey was ready with a large fleet. In the Battle of Leyte Gulf, the Japanese lost most of their remaining ships. After the Philippine campaign, Iwo Jima and Okinawa fell after bitter fighting. Now, B-29 bombers could easily reach the mainland of Japan.

The Manhattan Project

In 1939, the United States began to develop an atomic bomb. The secret project was code-named the "Manhattan Project". After a test of the weapon in July 1945, President Truman approved the use of the bomb on Japanese targets, and Hiroshima was selected. On August 6, 1945, a B-29 dropped the bomb. As a giant mushroom cloud arose, a crew member said, "My God, what have we done?" When no offer to surrender came, the second and last bomb was dropped on Nagasaki on August 9. The Japanese surrendered on September 2, 1945, on the battleship *Missouri,* in a ceremony presided over by General MacArthur. With the signing of the surrender papers, World War II came to an end.

Name: _____ Date: _____

Atomic Blasts End World War II: Activity

Directions: Go online to <https://www.youtube.com/watch?v=4EqRTWMVqMY> and view the Japanese Sign Final Surrender—1945 video clip. Then write your responses on the lines below.

1. Write the opening sentence of General MacArthur's speech.

    _____

    _____

    _____

    _____

2. Write General MacArthur's closing remarks.

    _____

    _____

    _____

    _____

3. Explain how the film contributes to your understanding of the reading selection. Support your answer with examples or details.

    _____

    _____

    _____

    _____

    _____

    _____

    _____

The United States Faces New Economic Challenges

Harry S Truman Becomes President

A good deal of uncertainty swept the United States at the end of World War II. Adding to the tension was the fact that the nation had a new president, Harry S Truman, who assumed the office on April 12, 1945, after Franklin Roosevelt died. On him fell tremendous national and international policy decisions, and there was reason to doubt that he was up to the job. A farm boy from Missouri, he had served in World War I as an artillery captain, then returned to Kansas City where he opened a men's clothing store. When the business failed, he got into Jackson County politics. Elected senator in 1934 and 1940, he voted for New Deal legislation. In 1944, he was chosen as vice president to replace the unpopular Henry Wallace. With no college education, no foreign policy experience, and no domestic policy-making positions on his credentials, there was reason to question his ability.

Harry S Truman

America After the War Ends

Certain forces were at work after World War II: (1) A great consumer demand had built up. People had saved money, but there was little for them to buy during the war. Now they needed to replace their car, refrigerator, and furniture, or to buy one of the new consumer items on the market: televisions, freezers, air conditioners, and hi-fis, (2) Thousands of soldiers, sailors, and marines were anxious to return to their civilian lives. If all of them entered the job market at the same time, unemployment would be serious again. (3) American producers realized Office of Price Administration (OPA) price controls would soon be lifted, and once that happened, they could get a higher price for their goods. (4) Workers had lived with wage controls during the war, but now they demanded higher wages.

The military forces were quickly reduced from 12.5 million to 3 million in 1946, and to 1.5 million in 1947. To keep all these veterans from entering the job market at the same time, the GI Bill was passed in 1944. It paid educational benefits for veterans to attend colleges and trade schools and gave generous loans to buy homes or start new businesses.

When OPA collapsed in 1946, higher prices hit the nation, which triggered inflation and a series of labor strikes. When the United Mine Workers (UMW) strike had lasted 40 days, an impatient Truman ordered that the government seize the mines. The miners went back to work a week later. When railway unions went out on strike, Truman asked Congress for power to draft workers. The unions gave in to the pressure, but Truman's popularity was dropping. "To err is Truman," was a phrase often heard.

What Were the Results?

Public pressure was strong after the war to move to a peacetime economy, but many demands were shortsighted and later aroused public wrath. Truman had the slogan on his desk "The buck stops here," but business, labor unions, farmers, and the general public had to accept their share of the blame.

Name: _____ Date: _____

The United States Faces New Economic Challenges: Activity

Directions: Think about what you have read, then answer the questions below. Support your answer with details and examples from the reading selection.

1. Why did people question Truman's ability to serve as president?

2. What issues were facing the United States after World War II?

3. How did President Truman handle labor strikes?

The United States Assumes a World Leader's Role

United Nations Established

After World War I, Wilson had tried to become a major player in world affairs but had been undercut by the Senate and American public opinion. As a former member of Wilson's Cabinet, President Franklin D. Roosevelt was vitally interested in the idea of an international organization to settle disputes before they turned into wars. In 1944, nations involved in the war against Japan and Germany held meetings in Washington to create the United Nations. The new organization would have a General Assembly (each member with one vote), and a Security Council of eleven members (five permanent: United States, England, France, U.S.S.R., and China). Each Security Council member had veto power. Roosevelt avoided Woodrow Wilson's mistakes by allowing both Republicans and senators to attend U.N. organizational meetings.

Hopes for a stable world after the war depended on the great powers cooperating with each other, but that hope faded quickly after the war. Trouble between the United States and Russia had actually begun during the war, when Stalin suspected that the United States and England were ganging up on him. At the Yalta conference in February 1945, Stalin, Churchill, and Roosevelt discussed the postwar world. By that time, Russian troops were already in Eastern Europe (Poland, Czechoslovakia, eastern Germany), so Roosevelt was in a poor bargaining position; but Stalin did agree to allow "free elections" in Poland and said Russia would enter the war against Japan two or three months after the war in Europe ended. Two months later, Roosevelt died.

Formation of East and West Germany

The new president, Harry Truman, was angered when the Russians set up communist governments in Eastern Europe without elections. So in July 1945, Truman, Stalin, and Churchill met at Potsdam, Germany, to discuss the military occupation and rebuilding of Germany. It became clear to Truman that it did no good to "appease" Stalin.

At the Yalta Conference, it had been agreed that Germany and Austria would each be divided into four zones, and that Berlin, although surrounded by East Germany, would also be divided into four zones. The Russians had quickly moved to set up a puppet government inside East Germany and the Soviet Zone in Austria. In 1946, the United States, England, and France merged their zones, and western Germany was dubbed "Trizonia." That move angered the Russians, who threatened to take West Berlin. In March of 1946, Churchill gave a post-war speech at a small college in Fulton, Missouri. In his speech, he said, "From Stettin in the Baltic to Trieste in the Adriatic, an iron curtain has descended across the Continent." This speech caused Americans to become concerned about the future intentions of Communist Russia.

New Agencies Are Created

In 1947, the United States made important changes. The War and Navy departments were merged into a new Department of Defense, and the Central Intelligence Agency (CIA) and the National Security Council (NSC) were formed to advise the president on foreign policy matters.

What Were the Results?

Unlike the reaction after World War I, the United States realized it had a responsibility to play the role of world leader. The new American awareness of global affairs was clearly shown by President Truman's speech to Congress on March 12, 1947. The policies of the Truman Doctrine were to "support free peoples who are resisting attempted subjugation by armed minorities or by outside pressures."

Name: _____   Date: _____

The United States Assumes a World Leader's Role: Activity

Directions: Use information from the reading selection to complete the graphic organizer.

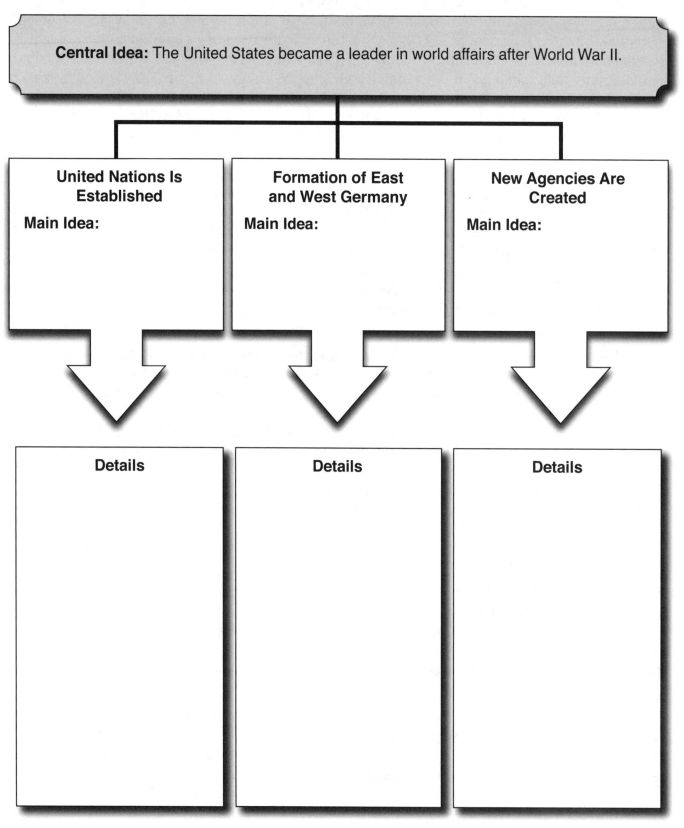

Central Idea: The United States became a leader in world affairs after World War II.

United Nations Is Established	Formation of East and West Germany	New Agencies Are Created
Main Idea:	**Main Idea:**	**Main Idea:**

Details	Details	Details

The Expansion of Communism in Asia

Communists in China

While most American attention focused on Europe, there was also concern over Communist advances in Asia. The United States backed the Chinese Nationalists led by Chiang Kai-Shek, who was trying to fight off Mao Zedong's Communists. Because the outcome would seriously affect the Cold War, President Truman sent General George C. Marshall to China to work out a truce and to persuade both sides to set up a coalition government. His effort failed because of hard-liners on both sides, Mao's belief that he would win, and the corruption and unpopularity of Chiang. In 1949, Chiang and his army fled to Taiwan. Many nations, including Great Britain and Russia, recognized the Communist government set up in Peking. The United States refused.

Chiang's collapse presented a difficult international problem. Who was to represent China in the United Nations? The United States insisted the Nationalist government was still the legitimate representative of the Chinese people and used its power to prevent a switch in representation.

U.S. Supports South Korea

Korea presented an unusual problem. It was divided at the 38th parallel in the closing days of World War II as a temporary arrangement. As time passed, two separate governments were set up—the one to the north was a Russian ally, while the South Korean government was an American ally.

On June 25, 1950, North Korean troops attacked South Korea without warning, and Truman made some quick decisions. Without consulting Congress, he committed American air, naval, and land forces to support South Korea. The U.N. Security Council condemned the attack, and General Douglas MacArthur was appointed to lead U.N. forces in Korea. A few nations, notably Turkey, sent troops to help in the war, but it was basically an American effort.

MacArthur Relieved of His Command

MacArthur was able to stabilize the line around the "Pusan Beachhead" and stage a dramatic landing on the west coast of Korea at Inchon. Many North Korean troops quickly surrendered, and the war moved north of the 38th parallel. England and France feared the United States was overcommitted in Asia now, and they worried that Russia might use this as an opportunity to threaten Europe. They also warned that since the front had now moved so far north, China might enter the war. Truman discussed that possibility with MacArthur on Wake Island, and was assured that China would not get involved. MacArthur was wrong, and in November 1950, Chinese troops crossed the line, and the war was suddenly much enlarged.

MacArthur was never one to be silent and had made public statements that he could win the war if he could bomb Manchuria and bring in Chinese Nationalist troops to help with the fighting. MacArthur ignored Truman's orders to cease in these public protests. In April 1951, President Truman relieved MacArthur of his command. Truman's popularity crashed to new lows, but in Congressional hearings, General Omar Bradley defended the decision.

What Were the Results?

Truce talks began in July 1951, at Panmunjom, but progress was slow. It was not until after Eisenhower became president that the Chinese and Koreans stopped stalling and the war ended. The Korean War stopped Communist expansion in Korea, but it cost about 25,000 American lives and the Democrats much popularity.

Name: _____   Date: _____

The Expansion of Communism in Asia: Activity

Directions: Use information from the reading selection to complete the graphic organizer.

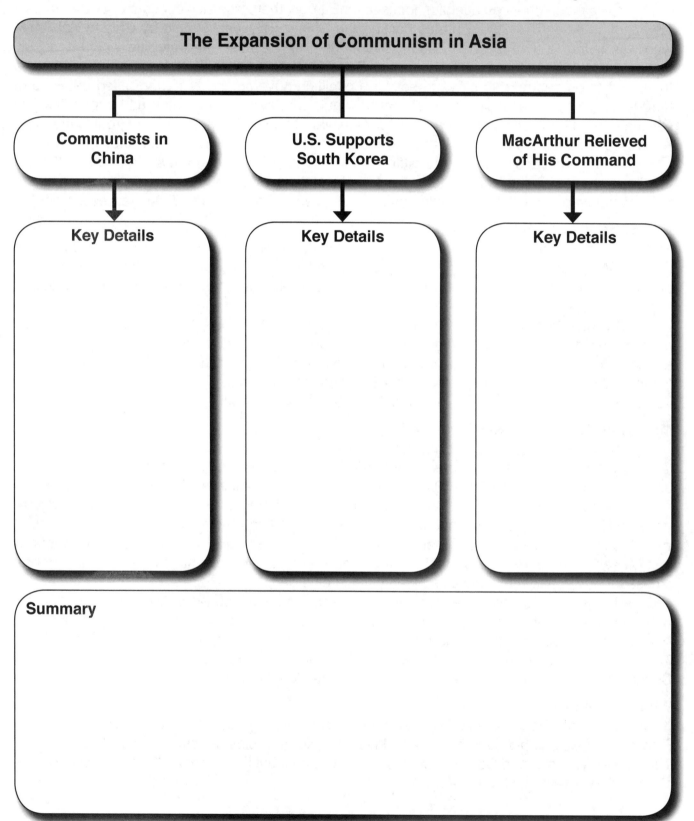

The Expansion of Communism in Asia

Communists in China	U.S. Supports South Korea	MacArthur Relieved of His Command
Key Details	Key Details	Key Details

Summary

McCarthyism Sweeps the Nation

The Rise of McCarthyism

On February 9, 1950, Wisconsin Senator Joe McCarthy spoke at the Republican Women's Club in Wheeling, West Virginia. Waving a piece of paper, he charged that there were 279* card-carrying communists in the State Department. That speech marked the beginning of a brief period known as the McCarthy Era, when anyone who had ever joined a communist organization, even if only briefly, feared exposure, character assassination, loss of income, and disgrace. McCarthy did not start the "Red Scare," but he used fear and frustration to the hilt.

Since the beginning of the Cold War, it seemed that communism was on the march all over the world. Worse, had communist sympathizers gained high positions in government, by which they could destroy the government of the United States? How did the Russians develop the atomic bomb by 1949? Were American scientists passing on secrets?

The House Un-American Activities Committee

In 1947, the House Un-American Activities Committee (HUAC) looked into accusations made against certain members of the film industry. After a Communist Party leader, Eugene Dennis, was charged with conspiring against the United States, the Supreme Court upheld his conviction because: "certain kinds of speech are so undesirable as to warrant criminal prosecution." The spy trial of Julius and Ethel Rosenberg, charged with delivering atomic secrets to Russian agents, ended with a guilty verdict and their execution. In 1948, Alger Hiss, a former State Department official, was accused of being a Soviet spy. He faced a full hearing before the HUAC.

Attacking Communists Makes Headlines

McCarthy discovered that attacking communists made headlines, and it gave him a fame he had never had before. He was like a shotgun blasting at anything suspicious. If the target was guilty, that was great; if he ruined an innocent man, he could live with that. Among those he attacked were General George Marshall, General Dwight Eisenhower, Senator Millard Tydings, Secretary of State Dean Acheson, Dr. J. Robert Oppenheimer (father of the atomic bomb), Protestant ministers, the U.S. Information Agency, and those in the executive branch who refused to turn over classified documents to him.

President Truman occasionally spoke out against him but then conducted security checks of government employees. President Eisenhower refused "to get in the gutter with *that* guy" but quietly began undermining him.

The Senate Censures McCarthy

When McCarthy charged that there were communists in the army, the army challenged him. Televised hearings were held, and for most Americans who had only recently bought their TV sets, this was great drama. The hearings left the impression that McCarthy was an arrogant bully who could dish it out but rambled and asked for points of order when he was questioned. In December 1954, the Senate censured (formally disapproved) McCarthy; he died three years later. McCarthy, like many politicians, was looking for a gimmick to use in his next campaign. If his effort had been to find truly dangerous traitors within the government, his search might have been beneficial, but it would have been short. In threatening freedom of speech, he did more harm to American democracy than any communists he found.

*Some sources say 279, 205, or 81; no one is exactly sure of which figure McCarthy used that day. His lack of specifics should have raised some suspicion at the time, but it did not.

Name: _____   Date: _____

McCarthyism Sweeps the Nation: Activity

Directions: Use information from the reading selection to complete the graphic organizer.

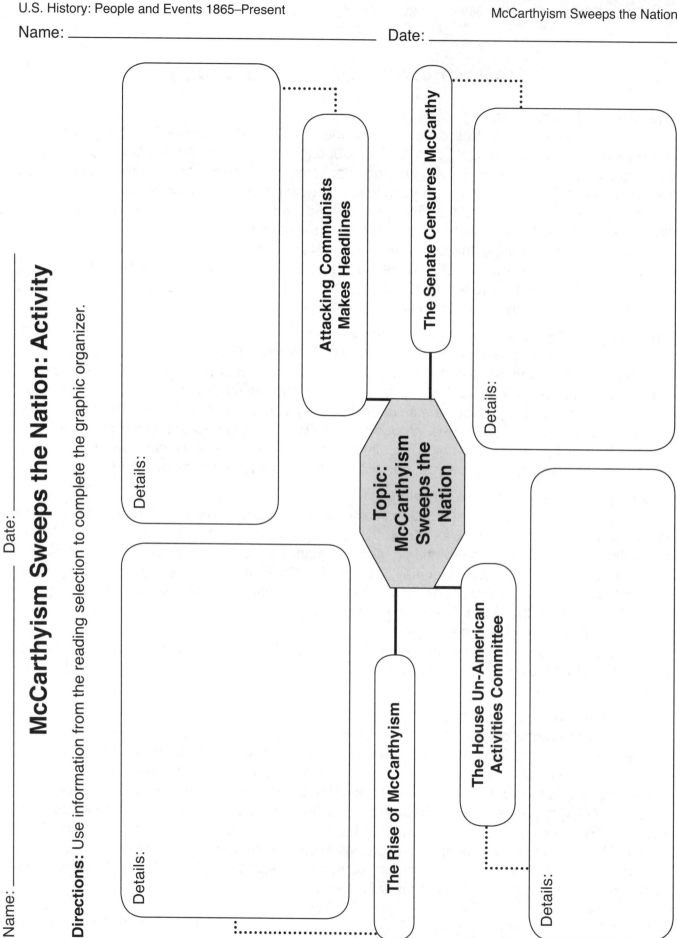

Details:

Attacking Communists Makes Headlines

The Senate Censures McCarthy

Details:

Topic: McCarthyism Sweeps the Nation

Details:

The Rise of McCarthyism

The House Un-American Activities Committee

Details:

Desegregation in America

Conservative white southerners were alarmed by the "sweeping changes" they saw in the late 1940s and early 1950s. An African-American player, Jackie Robinson, broke baseball's color line in 1947. A civil rights plank (goal) passed at the 1948 Democratic presidential convention. The armed service integration started in 1948. The *Brown v. Board of Education* Supreme Court case decision in 1954 denounced segregation in schools, and the border states began desegregating. Then in 1956, an African-American group in Montgomery, Alabama, organized a city bus boycott after Rosa Parks refused to give up her seat to a white man. Even the arrest of the boycott's leader, Martin Luther King, Jr., did not slow the protest.

Resistance to these changes was growing. White Citizens Councils formed to use economic and political pressure on those willing to change the system. If that did not work, the muscle of the Ku Klux Klan could be applied. In March 1957, 100 members of Congress signed the "Southern Manifesto," pledging to use all legal means to stop desegregation.

Eisenhower Backs Desegregation

President Eisenhower, who had backed desegregation of schools and public accommodations in the District of Columbia, continued desegregating the armed forces. He also pressured Congress to pass the Civil Rights Bill of 1957, which authorized the Department of Justice to prosecute any official denying African Americans the right to vote. Still, southern conservatives felt Eisenhower was not enthused about putting the full weight of federal power into supporting the *Brown* decision. Privately, he felt that no law or Supreme Court decision could change the "hearts and minds of men."

Little Rock

In the Arkansas capital of Little Rock, the school board voted to allow nine African-American students to attend Central High School in 1957. When Governor Orval Faubus did nothing to protest, a group of white mothers visited with him and warned that his political future was in danger unless he stopped the racial mixing. He responded by calling out the National Guard and ordering them to prevent the nine students from entering the building. Many efforts were made by government officials to change Faubus's mind, and even a meeting with Eisenhower failed to make the governor cooperate. After a court order, Faubus withdrew the National Guard, which left protection of the African-American students in the hands of the Little Rock police.

Each day, large, noisy, and hostile crowds from all over the South gathered outside the high school, and the police had no choice except to move the African-American students out a back entrance to prevent violence.

Eisenhower had had enough of this defiance of federal courts. He took command of the Arkansas National Guard and ordered them to protect the African-American students. He added 1,000 paratroopers, and the guardsmen and soldiers kept the crowd away with bayonets. As soon as possible, federal troops were withdrawn, but the Guard stayed until school ended in May.

In 1958, Faubus closed the Little Rock schools, but by 1959, the people of Little Rock demanded that the schools be reopened. President Eisenhower made it clear that governors must obey federal court orders, even if most white constituents disagreed with them. Still, progress was very slow. By 1960, only 50 African Americans in North Carolina and four in Louisiana attended school with white students.

Name: _____ Date: _____

Desegregation in America: Activity

Directions: Complete the graphic organizer using information from the reading selection.

Question   **Answer**

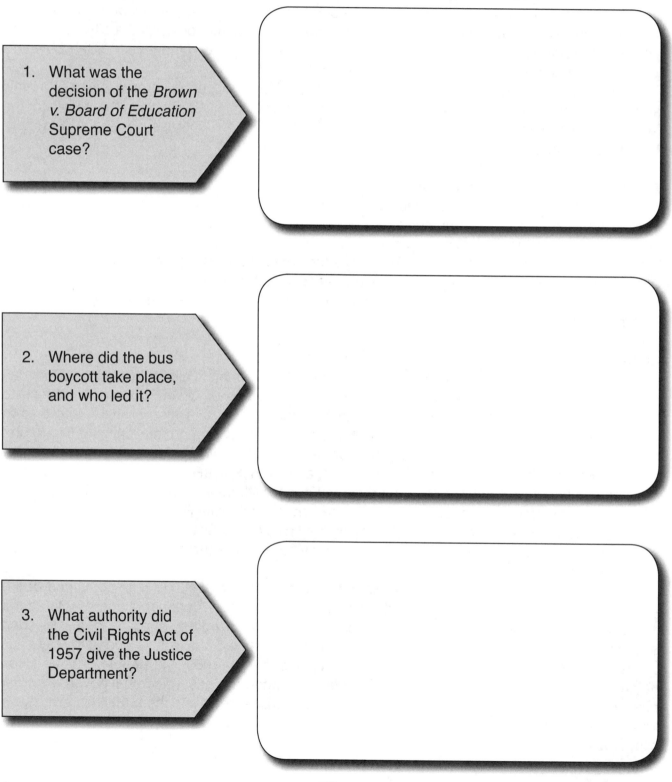

1. What was the decision of the *Brown v. Board of Education* Supreme Court case?

2. Where did the bus boycott take place, and who led it?

3. What authority did the Civil Rights Act of 1957 give the Justice Department?

The Cuban Missile Crisis

Communism in Cuba

As a senator, John F. Kennedy often criticized the foreign policies of the Truman and Eisenhower administrations. He felt the policies failed to stop communism's spread, and one of his prime examples was Fidel Castro's takeover of Cuba. In 1959, Castro had overthrown the corrupt dictator, Fulgencio Batista, and had begun trading with Russia. After American oil companies in Cuba refused to refine Russian crude oil, Castro took over the refineries. Defying the United States gave Castro great prestige among many Latin Americans.

U-2 Spy Plane Incident

Tension between the United States and the United Soviet Socialist Republic (U.S.S.R) was elevated. Plans were made to conduct a summit meeting in Paris between the U.S.S.R and western nations. The goal of the conference was to discuss disarmament, and hopefully, ease tensions between the two superpowers. However, on May 1, 1960, an American U-2 spy plane was shot down deep within Russia, and its pilot, Gary Powers, was captured. The United States denied it was spying on Russia by claiming it was a weather plane. This was proven to be false. When President Eisenhower refused to apologize for the United States spying on the Soviet Union, Nikita Khrushchev, the Soviet leader, left the conference on the first day. The U-2 incident had ruined Eisenhower's dream of settling serious issues between the two nations. While Khrushchev at least respected Eisenhower, he considered the incoming president, John F. Kennedy, too young and inexperienced to be treated as an equal.

Conflict Between Two Superpowers

Competition between the two superpowers continued to run strong. The Russians were far ahead of the United States in their space program. President Kennedy vowed that the United States would beat the Russians to the moon and persuaded Congress to put billions of dollars into the effort. The United States gave support to South Vietnam, sending not only money but the Green Berets, to train their army. Kennedy also sent an army of U.S.-trained Cuban refugees to liberate their homeland from Castro. The spot chosen for the attack was the Bay of Pigs, but the effort was a total failure. The men were killed or rounded up, and Castro held them as hostages until the United States paid $53 million for their return. Castro's influence rose in Latin America, while U.S. prestige dropped.

Cuban Missile Crisis

Khrushchev saw weakness in the American president and again threatened Berlin. President Kennedy called up 250,000 reservists, and Khrushchev backed down, but he built the Berlin Wall to prevent any more East Germans from escaping to the West. In October 1962, U-2 flights over Cuba revealed that missile launch pads were being built. Kennedy had to move quickly before the missiles already there could be put in place or ships carrying more missiles could arrive in Cuba. In a televised speech, he told the nation a "quarantine line" had been placed around Cuba, and U.S. ships would stop any Russian ship that appeared to be carrying missiles. World War III was a distinct possibility. Feeling the pressure, Khrushchev backed down; the missiles were crated up, and Russian ships with missiles aboard returned to Russia.

The Cuban missile crisis caused Kennedy's popularity to rise dramatically. Khrushchev's power in Russia declined. The United States denied that it was part of the deal, but it took some missiles out of Turkey and promised never to invade Cuba again.

The Cuban Missile Crisis: Activity

Directions: Use information from the reading selection to complete the graphic organizers.

Topic: U-2 Spy Plane Incident	**Key Details**
Summary	

Topic: Cuban Missile Crisis	**Key Details**
Summary	

The Vietnam War

The War in the 1950s

No war in American history stirred up so much controversy as did the war in Vietnam. It began as a civil war between the Vietminh guerrillas and the colonial government of French Indo-China. Ho Chi Minh, leader of the rebels, was very successful despite the large amount of U.S. military aid going to help the French. By 1954, the French had lost the northern part and agreed to divide Vietnam at the 17th parallel. Worried about the "domino effect" (if one nation falls, those around it will fall), the United States and friends met and formed the Southeast Asia Treaty Organization (SEATO), which promised to consult with any nation threatened by aggression or subversion. Eisenhower sent military aid, but no American troops.

Gulf of Tonkin Resolution

President Kennedy became concerned about the growing power of the Vietcong (South Vietnamese rebels) and sent 16,000 American "military advisers" to help South Vietnam resist. After Kennedy's assassination, President Johnson faced the unpleasant reality that unless the United States acted soon, the "rice basket of Asia" would be lost. The Republican presidential candidate in 1964, Barry Goldwater, criticized the no-win war in Vietnam and urged that we become fully involved. Johnson said it was an Asian war, not ours; but in August 1964, that changed. Using the reported attack of three North Vietnamese patrol boats on an American destroyer as justification, he urged Congress to pass the Gulf of Tonkin resolution to permit him to use "all necessary measures" to "repel any armed attack" and prevent "future aggression." It easily passed in Congress.

Public Opinion and the Draft

After Johnson's decisive victory in the 1964 election, the United States became deeply committed to the war in Vietnam. Thousands of young men were drafted to fight in a different type of war without front lines and against enemies who set different types of traps, then blended back into the jungles.

Some young men avoided the war by getting college deferments. Anti-war movements began on college campuses among idealists and those fearing their deferments would end before the war did. Some avoided the draft by moving to Canada, and others defied the government by burning their draft cards. Anti-war feeling even grew among the soldiers fighting the war. Public opinion was divided on the war, and that split was obvious in Congress. In the Senate, J. William Fulbright led the "doves" (those urging withdrawal), and Barry Goldwater led the "hawks" (those wanting to do whatever it took to win). Adding pressure was taxpayer discontent with an expensive war.

After President Johnson assured the public that the war was nearly won, the Tet Offensive (January 1968) proved it was not. His popularity dropped so low that he did not seek another term as president.

Nixon and Ford Era

Hostility to the war became even stronger during the Nixon and Ford era. On April 23, 1975, in a speech at Tulane University in New Orleans, President Gerald Ford announced, the Vietnam War "is finished as far as America is concerned." The war ended on April 30, 1975, when the last American troops left Saigon. At the time, many felt Vietnam was an experience to forget, and those returning home from the war felt bitter and defeated.

Name: _____ Date: _____

The Vietnam War: Activity

Directions: Paraphrase each section of the Joint Resolution excerpt from the Gulf of Tonkin Resolution.

Gulf of Tonkin Resolution	Paraphrase (restate in your own words)
(1) Joint Resolution To promote the maintenance of international peace and security in southeast Asia.	
(2) Whereas naval units of the Communist regime in Vietnam, in violation of the principles of the Charter of the United Nations and of international law, have deliberately and repeatedly attacked United States naval vessels lawfully present in international waters, and have thereby created a serious threat to international peace; and	
(3) Whereas these attackers are part of deliberate and systematic campaign of aggression that the Communist regime in North Vietnam has been waging against its neighbors and the nations joined with them in the collective defense of their freedom; and	
(4) Whereas the United States is assisting the peoples of southeast Asia to protect their freedom and has no territorial, military or political ambitions in that area, but desires only that these people should be left in peace to work out their destinies in their own way: Now, therefore be it	
(5) *Resolved by the Senate and House of Representatives of the United States of America in Congress assembled,* That the Congress approves and supports the determination of the President, as Commander in Chief, to take all necessary measures to repel any armed attack against the forces of the United States and to prevent further aggression.	

1968–A Tragic Year

By 1968, conservatives were loudly complaining about civil rights protesters, anti-war demonstrators, "women's libbers," and those favoring an end to obscenity, drug, and alcohol laws. The TV family of the 1950s with its wise mom and dad had been replaced in the 1960s by parents who were no match for wise-cracking offspring. Polite manners in the workplace and on buses were now seen as "male chauvinism." Respect for police was replaced by insulting name calling. Business was under attack for polluting air, requiring ties and dresses, and placing greed over community needs. The flag was being burned at campus protests while men were dying for their country in Vietnam.

Supreme Court Decisions

Some blamed this atmosphere on Earl Warren and the Supreme Court. In 1962, the Court banned prayer in public schools, and the next year it banned Bible reading. The *Gideon v. Wainwright*, decision required that a state provide an attorney for the accused, if he could not afford to pay for his own defense. The *Miranda v. Arizona* decision required that a person must be informed of his rights before questioning began. The Court also restricted a community's right to ban objectionable books and movies. "Impeach Earl Warren" signs began to appear in many parts of the country.

Election of 1968

President Johnson's "Great Society" seemed more like a "fractured society." Johnson barely won the New Hampshire primary in March 1968 against the little-known senator, Eugene McCarthy. Then Robert Kennedy, the younger brother of former President John Kennedy, entered the primary race. President Johnson, realizing he had little chance for reelection, announced he would not seek a second term. With support from party leaders, Vice President Hubert Humphrey became a Democratic primary candidate.

> **Did You Know?**
>
> The "Great Society" was a group of programs during the Johnson administration that mainly focused on eliminating poverty and racial injustice in the United States.

On April 4, 1968, in Memphis, Tennessee, the Rev. Martin Luther King, Jr., a civil rights advocate who promoted racial harmony and non-violence, was shot and killed. A rampage of looting and burning broke out in 125 cities. Then, on June 6 in Los Angeles, California, Robert Kennedy was killed while he and his supporters were celebrating his victory in the California primary.

The Yippies, a counterculture group, announced their intention to disrupt the Democratic National Convention in August. Chicago's Mayor Richard Daley warned that it was not going to happen in his town. While delegates met behind barbed-wire fences, the police battled with demonstrators in the streets. A badly divided party chose Humphrey as their candidate.

Richard Nixon was chosen as the Republican nominee and drew support from many traditional conservatives. George Wallace, former governor of Alabama, appealed to the working class and poor whites as the American Independent candidate. Nixon and Wallace both promised that if elected, they would do whatever was necessary to restore order.

It appeared at first that Nixon would win easily, but Humphrey surged toward the end; however, in the popular vote Nixon received 31.7 million votes to Humphrey's 31.2 million. Nixon won the presidency easily in the Electoral College. The combined votes for Nixon and Wallace were 41.1 million, signaling the public was ready for a conservative solution to America's problems.

Name: _____   Date: _____

1968—A Tragic Year: Activity

Directions: Research one of the names listed in the box. Then complete the activity.

Richard Daley	Robert Kennedy	Richard Nixon
Hubert Humphrey	Martin Luther King, Jr.	George Wallace
Lyndon Johnson	Eugene McCarthy	Earl Warren

Biographical Research

Person: _____

Birth Date: _____

Place of Birth: _____

Positions Held in Government: _____

_____

_____

_____

_____

Important/Notable Contributions: _____

_____

_____

_____

_____

_____

_____

_____

President Richard Nixon and Watergate

Richard M. Nixon

Richard Nixon's first term was far more tranquil than Johnson's had been. Nixon quickly reduced the U.S. military force in Vietnam to 50,000, which meant fewer men being drafted. Strongly anti-communist in his early years, he and his chief foreign policy advisor, Henry Kissinger, worked toward *detente*, a relaxing of tension, between the United States and the U.S.S.R. He opened diplomatic relations with communist China and visited Chairman Mao in Peking. National pride ran high when the American flag was planted on the moon on July 21, 1969.

To the surprise of many, Nixon pushed two new agencies: the Environmental Protection Agency (EPA) and the Occupational Safety and Health Administration (OSHA). He approved increasing social security benefits, a reform of the tax system, and federal aid to low- and middle-income home buyers. When the economy became sluggish, he started spending more money; when inflation came, he put on price and wage controls.

Not everyone was happy, though. African-American leaders found him opposed to busing students to achieve integration. The anti-war movement was still strong, and it wanted all American troops out of Vietnam. Many did not trust Nixon, and reporters were unhappy with the devoted followers who surrounded the president.

Watergate Leads to Nixon's Resignation

The 1972 election was an easy victory for Nixon, who received over 60 percent of the popular vote and won 520–17 in electoral votes. Few had believed George McGovern's charge that the five burglars caught at the Democratic National Committee's headquarters inside the Watergate complex in Washington D.C., were in fact agents of the Committee to Reelect the President (CREEP). Judge John Sirica, who tried the men, sentenced them to 20 years in prison. Jim McCord, one of the defendants, told the judge that higher officials in CREEP were involved. Two *Washington Post* reporters, Bob Woodward and Carl Bernstein, were fed information about a cover-up from a secret source. Then a Senate committee chaired by Sam Ervin began an investigation, and Attorney General Elliot Richardson appointed a special prosecutor, Archibald Cox, to look into charges.

John Dean, a lawyer for Nixon, said he had been at White House meetings where a cover-up was discussed, and he included dates and times. Nixon denied wrongdoing, and the matter might have stopped there, except that it was discovered there was a taping machine in the Oval Office; Cox tried without success to get the tapes. During this controversy, Vice President Agnew was forced to resign because of bribes he had taken while governor of Maryland. Agnew was replaced by Gerald Ford.

Cox went to court to get the tapes, and Nixon ordered Richardson to fire him. When the attorney general refused, he was fired and so was the number-two man at the Justice Department. The number-three man fired Cox, but public outrage was so strong that a new prosecutor, Leon Jaworski, was appointed. After the Supreme Court ordered Nixon to turn over all the incriminating tapes, he was ruined. The House Judiciary Committee voted three charges of impeachment. Senate Republican leaders went to Nixon and told him, if he did not resign, he would most certainly be impeached. Nixon resigned on August 9, 1974, and Vice President Ford became president. President Ford said, "Our long national nightmare is over."

Name: _____ Date: _____

President Richard Nixon and Watergate: Activity

Directions: Use information from the reading selection to answer the questions.

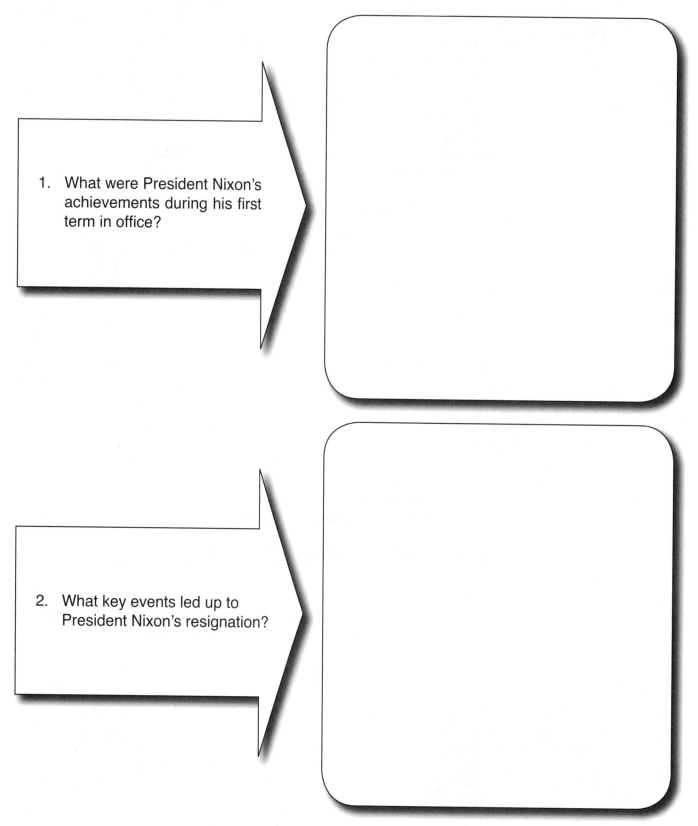

1. What were President Nixon's achievements during his first term in office?

2. What key events led up to President Nixon's resignation?

Celebration of the American Dream

On July 4, 1776, by act of the Second Continental Congress, the United States declared independence from England. Two hundred years later, 220 sailing ships ("tall ships" as they were now called) from 30 nations came to New York to help the United States celebrate 200 years of independence. From Maine to Hawaii, bands played, marchers paraded, and orators praised the founding fathers for their courage and vision.

In the first 200 years of independence, the accomplishments of the American people far exceeded the wildest dreams of the founders. Fifty states, instead of 13, extended from Maine to Hawaii, from Florida to Alaska. There were over 200 million Americans whose ancestors came from virtually every nation on Earth. Mines, factories, farms, and businesses were among the most productive in the world. Then, it took weeks for some delegates to reach Philadelphia; 200 years later, they could have made the trip in a few hours. A people on the edge of world affairs had moved to the center of the world stage.

Honoring the American Dream

Something was missing, however. The United States was not feeling good about itself. It had failed to live up to the Pledge of Allegiance's "one nation, under God, indivisible…" The Kerner Commission had reported in 1967, "Our nation is moving toward two societies, one black, one white—separate but unequal." The Declaration of Independence's goal of "life, liberty and the pursuit of happiness" had not reached the poor and those lacking in education and job skills. The "domestic tranquility" had disappeared in urban riots. The failure in Vietnam sent an unwelcome surge of humility into a nation that had boasted of its past military successes and technological superiority. Watergate was still painfully fresh in the memory of Americans. Something had gone very wrong with the American dream.

This was the challenge of 1976 or any other year. The fault was not in the dream, but in the failure of people to remember and honor the dream—to keep working toward goals that always seemed beyond reach. When quantity replaces quality, when the easy is preferred over the right, when judgment is based on a person's skin color rather than his heart and mind, when people make decisions based only on present whims rather than future goals, the dream is postponed.

The Rule of Law Prevails

Yet, there was also reason to believe that the dream was not forgotten. When the Supreme Court ruled against President Nixon, he obeyed the ruling and turned over the tapes. The rule of law was alive and well. President Ford would have differences with Congress, but they never feared arrest in the middle of the night and continued to challenge his vetoes without fear of reprisal. In 1976, Democrat Jimmy Carter ran against Republican Gerald Ford and won. No effort was made to call off the election because of a "national emergency," no ballots were burned, no voters threatened. When President Ford lost, he conceded defeat, and the transition process toward a new administration began. The federal government, despite its flaws, still worked.

"City Upon a Hill"

The newly arrived Asians, the Cuban refugees, and the thousands of others who came to the United States from around the world in the 1970s saw an opportunity in America to achieve a new and better life for themselves and their children. The challenge to native-born Americans and immigrants alike was to become John Winthrop's "city upon a hill." The eyes of all people are still upon us.

Name: _____ Date: _____

Celebration of the American Dream: Activity

Directions: Think about what you have learned from the reading selection. Then reflect on your dream for America's future. Write your reflection on the lines below.

My Dream for America's Future

_____

_____

_____

_____

_____

_____

_____

_____

_____

_____

_____

_____

_____

_____

_____

_____

_____

_____

President Ronald Reagan

In 1981, Ronald Wilson Reagan was inaugurated as the 40th president of the United States. At 69 years old, he was the oldest man to serve as president. A former actor, Reagan was comfortable giving speeches and being in front of a camera. His outstanding public speaking skills earned him the nickname "The Great Communicator."

Ronald Reagan

Path to the White House

Ronald Reagan was born on February 6, 1911, in Tampico, Illinois. His parents were John and Nelle Reagan. He graduated from high school and then worked his way through college. He married Jane Wyman, an actress, in 1940, but they later divorced. In 1952, he married Nancy Davis, also an actress.

Reagan had several successful careers before entering politics. He was a radio sports announcer, an actor, and a television host. He left acting and turned to politics. He served two terms as governor of California (1967–1971) but declined to run for a third term. He made two unsuccessful attempts for the Republican presidential nomination in 1968 and 1976. Finally, in 1980, he was nominated as the Republican candidate for president. In the presidential election, he went on to defeat Democratic candidate President Jimmy Carter, who was seeking his second term in office.

Shortly after taking office in 1981, John Hinckley made an assassination attempt on Reagan's life. Several shots were fired, wounding President Reagan and three other people. Hinckley was later found not guilty by reason of insanity and placed under institutional psychiatric care.

Domestic Policy

Reagan promised his voters a conservative domestic policy. His economic policy nicknamed "Reaganomics" was a plan to reduce government spending, taxes, government regulation, and inflation. The impact of these policies on the economy was mostly favorable; however, the national debt increased significantly during this time. By the end of Reagan's second term in office in 1989, the United States had entered a time of prosperity.

Foreign Policy

President Reagan stated his foreign policy was "peace through strength." Using this strategy, he negotiated an intermediate-range nuclear missiles treaty with the Soviet Union. He bombed Libya after they attacked American soldiers in a West Berlin nightclub. He sent naval support to the Persian Gulf to guarantee that oil flow would not be interrupted during the Iran-Iraq war. He gave support to anti-communist insurgencies in Central America, Asia, and Africa. In 1987, Reagan spoke at Germany's Berlin Wall. Speaking for the reunification of Germany, he demanded that Soviet Leader Mikhail Gorbachev "tear down this wall!" More than two years later, Gorbachev allowed the wall that had divided East and West Germany from 1961 to 1989 to be dismantled. Reagan's policy for achieving "peace through strength" seemed to be working.

Life After the Presidency

After leaving the White House, Reagan and his wife Nancy returned to their home in Bel Air, California. In 1994, it was announced that he was suffering from Alzheimer's disease. Ronald Reagan died on June 5, 2004, and was buried at his presidential library in California.

Name: _____ Date: _____

President Ronald Reagan: Activity

A former actor, President Reagan was comfortable giving speeches and being in front of a camera. His outstanding public speaking skills earned him the nickname "The Great Communicator."

Directions: Review the verbal and nonverbal delivery techniques below. Go online to the URL <https://www.youtube.com/watch?v=5MDFX-dNtsM> or search for another of President Reagan's speeches and observe him delivering his speech. As you watch the video, place a check mark next to any signals he uses. Then answer the questions below.

Verbal Signals	✔	Nonverbal Signals	✔
Diction The speaker pronounces words clearly so listeners can understand the presentation.		**Eye Contact** The speaker looks at the audience and makes eye contact with different members.	
Mood/Tone The presentation makes listeners feel certain emotions, which helps them to remember the main points presented.		**Facial Expressions** The speaker uses expressions such as smile, frown, or raised eyebrows. The expressions reinforce the words spoken.	
Pitch The speaker's voice rises and falls naturally when speaking.		**Body Movement** The speaker gestures with hand movements, shrugs, nods, and head movements. The gestures reinforce the message.	
Tempo/Volume The speaker slows down or pauses to emphasize key points. The speaker presents speech at a level that allows everyone to hear clearly.		**Posture** The speaker stands or sits tall and straight. The stance reflects or emphasizes the message.	

How did President Reagan's use of verbal and nonverbal signals enhance his message and engage the audience? Use details from the chart to support your answer.

_____

_____

_____

_____

A New Millennium

Americans approached the year 2000 with great excitement and a little worry. The start of a new millennium was an opportunity to dream of the coming advancements in science, medicine, and technology and reflect on the accomplishments of the past.

Since the Bicentennial celebrations of 1976, the computer had revolutionized business, communications, education, and daily life. The Internet, which had barely been known in 1976, now connected people all over the world. Medical technology had even allowed scientists to map the human genome by the year 2000, laying the foundation for further research in genetics, diseases, criminology, psychology, and many other disciplines.

Threat of Y2K

However, a small oversight built into many computers threatened to bring the fast-paced computer age to a halt as the clock struck midnight. It was feared that when the date changed to 01/01/2000, computers would not be able to process information, since they would interpret this date as an error. Programmers scrambled to fix the Y2K bug, as it was called, in order to avoid chaos in the world's computers. Whether due to the quick fix, an overestimation of the problem, or just good luck, very few problems were reported as the new millennium began.

Hope for Peace

Hope for peace was also strong as the nation looked toward the future. Communism had fallen apart in the Soviet Union during the presidencies of Ronald Reagan and George H.W. Bush. By 1990, Russia and the former Soviet-bloc countries in eastern Europe were independent nations. The Berlin Wall had been torn down, and democracy demonstrations had taken place in China. In 1991, the United States and other nations had fought together to keep the Iraqi leader Saddam Hussein from grabbing more land and power in the Middle East during the Persian Gulf War. The United States was also involved in peacekeeping missions in Somalia, Haiti, Kosovo, and other nations during the presidency of Bill Clinton. United States forces worked to stabilize countries torn apart by dictators, war lords, and civil war. Through these efforts, Americans hoped democracy could be spread over more of the world.

Unrest Grows in the Middle East

Growing unrest in the Middle East and other developing regions, however, constantly worked against those hopes. Assassinations and terrorist bombings in Israel, Palestinian-controlled lands, and African nations spurred world leaders to try to bring peace to the region and stop the continuing violence.

Terrorism at Home

While Americans were concerned about the violence in other nations, the trouble seemed far away. Most people did not worry about terrorist attacks in the United States. Violent incidents with extremist groups were very few. In fact, the largest terrorist attack in the United States had been committed by Americans Timothy McVeigh and Terry Nichols. They destroyed the federal building in Oklahoma City with a bomb on April 19, 1995, killing 168 men, women, and children.

Name: _____ Date: _____

A New Millennium: Activity

Directions: Use information from the reading selection to complete the graphic organizer.

Heading

Key Details

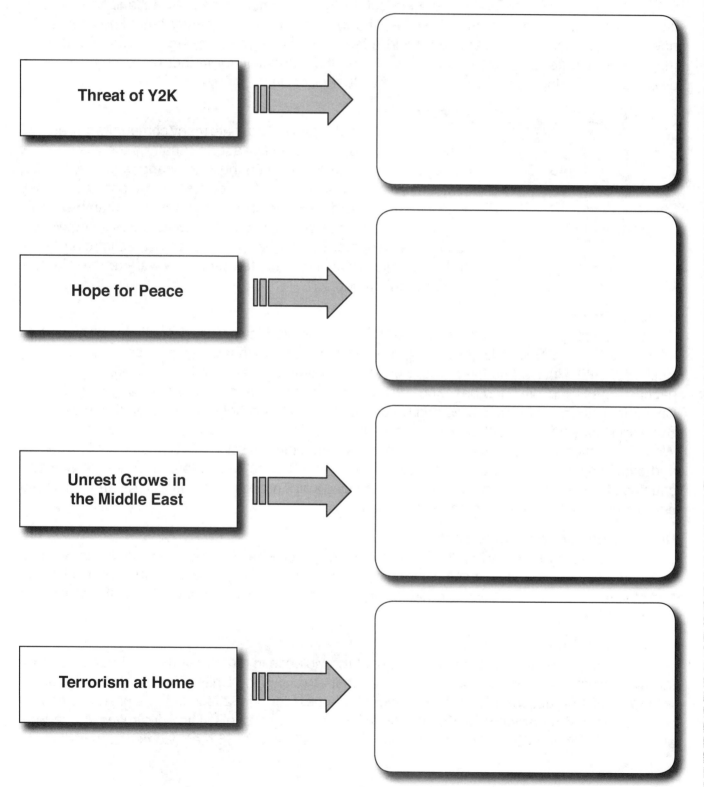

Threat of Y2K

Hope for Peace

Unrest Grows in
the Middle East

Terrorism at Home

A National Tragedy—September 11, 2001

No one could have predicted the attack on America that occurred on September 11, 2001. That morning, 19 Al Qaeda-trained terrorists launched a coordinated assault on the United States. Four commercial airliners were hijacked and used as aerial firebombs to destroy the Twin Towers of the World Trade Center in New York City and a section of the Pentagon in Washington, D.C. The fourth plane crashed in a Pennsylvania field, after heroic efforts by crew and passengers to retake control. The planes flown into the World Trade Center towers were loaded with fuel. The intense heat from the fires caused both buildings to collapse while office workers and rescuers were still trying to evacuate. Many other buildings in the area were also destroyed or damaged. During the attack, 2,986 people died as the world watched, shocked at the enormity of these attacks on American soil. This was the first full-scale enemy offensive conducted within the borders of the continental United States since the War of 1812. It was determined that the offensive was planned by Osama bin Laden and others supported by the Taliban dictatorship of Afghanistan and was executed by Al Qaeda (Islamic extremist group) terrorists. Their goals were to annihilate the government of the United States, to destroy the capitalist system of free enterprise, and to bring the 281 million citizens of the United States to  ruin. These terrorists were opposed to virtually everything the United States represents—freedom, equality, representation, and opportunity. Their militant version of Islamic "liberation" meant, quite simply, that those who did not submit to the word of Allah must die in a *jihad* (holy war).

George W. Bush Calls for an Attack on Terrorism

Within several weeks of the attacks, President George W. Bush announced that the United States would attack terrorism wherever it was uncovered. Afghanistan became the focus of military endeavors. A military alliance was formed with opposition forces in Afghanistan. Partnerships were cemented with Pakistan, China, Russia, Great Britain, and other world powers to isolate Afghanistan's dictatorship. The subsequent offensive resulted in the overthrow of the Taliban regime and the takeover of the country. Civilians, soldiers, and terrorists died in the process. American soldiers remained in Afghanistan to stabilize the country as it moved toward democracy and to try to capture Osama bin Laden and his followers.

U.S. Troops Invade Iraq

In 2003, when it appeared that there were ties between Osama bin Laden and Saddam Hussein, the leader of Iraq, President Bush ordered U.S. troops to invade Iraq. It was feared that the Iraqis had stockpiles of weapons of mass destruction, such as nuclear bombs or biological weapons, and would use them against neighboring nations or the United States. (This claim was later to be proven false.) American forces and their coalition allies quickly took Baghdad and other Iraqi cities. Saddam Hussein was captured on December 13, 2003. Most of the Iraqi people welcomed the Americans and their allies and were eager to be free of the corrupt government. However, many rebel insurgents from Iraq as well as other Islamic nations continued to fight because they resented the American presence. The insurgents used terrorist tactics such as car bombs, suicide bombs, and guerrilla attacks. Despite continuing unrest, both Afghanistan and Iraq held free, democratic elections in early 2005. Tensions in the Middle East would continue to increase, resulting in future terrorist threats throughout the world.

Name: _____ Date: _____

A National Tragedy—September 11, 2001

Directions: Conduct an oral history interview with someone who remembers the events surrounding September 11, 2001. If possible, create an audio or video recording of the interview.

Interview Questions

1. What is your name? _____

2. How old were you on September 11, 2001? _____

3. Where were you when you first heard about the events?

_____

_____

4. What do you remember about that day?

_____

_____

_____

_____

_____

5. What impact, if any, did the events of September 11, 2001, have on your life?

_____

_____

_____

_____

_____

President Barack Obama

On January 20, 2009, Barack Hussein Obama was inaugurated as the 44th president of the United States. The first African American to be elected president, President Obama believed "in the ability to unite people around a politics of purpose."

Election of 2008

On May 2, 2007, Barack Obama announced his candidacy to become the Democratic Party's presidential nominee. Many felt he was too inexperienced, since he was only in his first term as a U.S. senator from Illinois. He had a background in law, graduating from Harvard Law School in 1991 and teaching law classes at the University of Chicago. Despite doubts, he won the nomination on August 27, 2008, at the party's convention. On November 4, 2008, Barack Obama was elected as president of the United States, receiving almost 10,000,000 more popular votes than his Republican opponent, John McCain. His overwhelming win was credited to his proposals to deal with the economic crisis, his ability to get young voters to the polls, and outspending his opponent.

First Term in Office

When President Obama began his first term, he "inherited a troubled economic situation," often referred to as the Great Recession. In his inaugural address, he addressed the issues facing America, "Homes have been lost, jobs shed, businesses shuttered. Our health care is too costly, our schools fail too many..." To address these challenges, he said required "a new era of responsibility," in which Americans recognized and gladly seized the duties needed to face the "difficult task" ahead.

On February 17, 2009, he signed into law the American Recovery and Reinvestment Act (ARRA) a $787 billion economic-growth package that addressed tax cuts, infrastructure, energy, education, health care, and social welfare programs, such as an expansion of unemployment benefits. On March 23, 2010, he signed into law the Affordable Care Act (known as Obamacare), a plan to reform health care and cover millions of uninsured Americans. On July 21, 2010, he signed the Dodd-Frank Wall Street Reform and Consumer Protection Act, which reformed regulations of banking and financial institutions and created a consumer protection bureau.

Obama signed the instrument of ratification for a New START Treaty with Russia on February 2, 2011. The treaty limited the number of nuclear warheads and launchers and strengthened the monitoring program between the two countries. On May 2, 2011, he gave approval for special forces to raid the secret compound of and to kill Al Qaeda leader Osama bin Laden, the mastermind behind the September 11, 2001, terrorist attacks. Toward the end of his first term, he shifted the focus of America's military and foreign affairs to the Asian-Pacific region.

Second Term in Office

President Obama was reelected to a second term in office on November 6, 2012. In July 2015, the Iran Nuclear Deal was reached between Iran, the United States, and five other power nations. It limited Iran's nuclear capabilities. In October 2015, the unemployment rate dropped to 5%, and in December, he announced 13.7 million new jobs had been added "over a 69-month streak of growth." When President Obama left office, his approval rating was over 50%. The nation had gotten through the economic crisis, and the unemployment rate had dropped. However, his presidency was marked by a rise in racial tension and an increase in polarization between political parties.

Name: _____ Date: _____

President Barack Obama

Directions: Use information from the reading selection to develop a time line (from earliest to latest date) featuring events from President Obama's presidency. The first one is done for you.

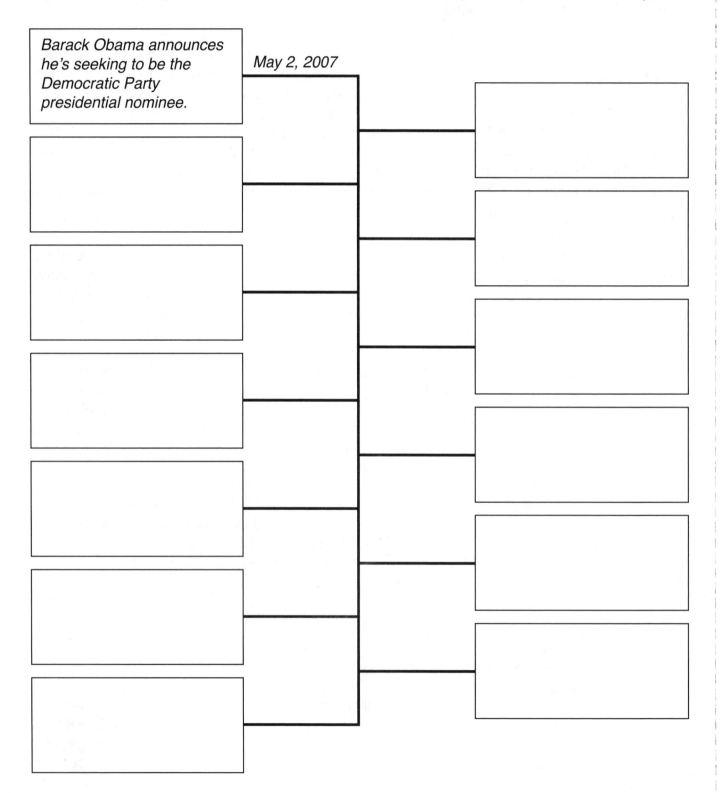

Barack Obama announces he's seeking to be the Democratic Party presidential nominee.

May 2, 2007

Answer Keys

Americans Face New Challenges: Activity (p. 6)

Independent Farmers: Before the war, many people owned and operated their own farms. After the war, America was a land of factories and stores with people working for employers and not for themselves.

Former Slaves: Former slaves were free but did not have full rights as citizens. They could not vote, hold public office, or sit on a jury.

Northern Soldiers: For Northern soldiers, finding a job after the war was difficult. They were entering the job market at the same time as millions of other soldiers.

Southern Soldiers: Many soldiers returned home with grave injuries. When they arrived, they were to find almost all they owned was lost: slaves, money, and property. There were no sheriffs, courts, or jails to keep Union and Confederate deserters from robbing and stealing.

President Andrew Johnson Is Impeached: Activity (p. 8)

Event 1: The nation went into a time of mourning. Andrew Johnson became president.

Event 2: He was often heckled and probably hurt the candidates he supported. When the opponents were elected, they had a two-thirds majority in both houses and could override his vetoes.

Event 3: A Cabinet member could not be removed without the consent of the Senate.

Event 4: The motion to remove Johnson as president failed by a single vote. Johnson finished his term and later returned to the Senate.

Reconstruction in the South: Activity (p. 10)

Problem 1: housing, clothing and feeding the millions of freed slaves

Solution: The Reconstruction plan established the Freedmen's Bureau to take care of the former slaves.

Problem 2: rebuilding the economy of the South

Solution: Reconstruction legislation funded railroad construction, building public schools, and set up new state constitutions.

Problem 3: uniting the Southern and Northern states under one government

Solution: Congress passed laws to establish new state governments. They called new constitutional conventions.

Corruption in Government: Activity (p. 12)

(Answers will vary but may include:)

Central Theme: Corruption during the Grant Administration

Observations: President Grant is holding up the other acrobats; the other acrobats can be identified by the names on their belts; the rings held by the other acrobats and the bells have words written on them

Symbols: *acrobat:* President Grant;

acrobat rings: Whiskey Ring and Navy Ring;

acrobat bar: 3rd term;

strap in acrobat's mouth: corruption of the administration

Summary: Whether intentional or not, the actions or inactions of President Grant supported, upheld, or allowed the corrupt actions of his political associates to happen.

The Transcontinental Railroad: Activity (p. 14)

(Answers will vary but may include:)

People: Chinese men

Objects: train engine and cars; mountains; shovels; forest; railroad tracks; tunnels; snow

Activities: Chinese men, some cheering, others standing or sitting watching train; smoke coming from train engine

Inference: The illustration shows the construction of the Central Pacific by the Chinese workers through the snowy Sierra Nevada Mountains.

Cattlemen Take Over the West's Rangeland: Activity (p. 16)

(Teacher verification is required.)

Custer's Last Stand: Activity (p. 18)

(Answers will vary.)

Who: Sioux, Cheyenne, Arapaho, George Armstrong Custer, and 265 soldiers

What: Custer and all of his 265 men were killed at the Battle of Little Bighorn.

When: June 25, 1876

Where: Little Bighorn Region in Montana

Why: In 1876, many Native Americans had left the reservation. The government ordered them to return by February 1. Instead of going back, many headed for the camp Sitting Bull and Crazy Horse had established on the Little Bighorn River. Custer had orders to search for Native Americans in the Little Bighorn region.

Sodbusters Invade the Great Plains: Activity (p. 20)

(Answers will vary but may include:)

1. There was a lack of trees. The sod could be cut into blocks and stacked like bricks to form a sod house.
2. Advantages: could be built quickly; stayed cool in summer and warm in winter
   Disadvantages: infested with insects, mice, and snakes; heavy spring rains caused them to leak
3. Answers will vary.

Growth of Business and Labor Unions: Activity (p. 22)

(Answers will vary but may include:)

Industrial Revolution

Main Idea: After the war there was a great growth in technology, which changed the way goods were manufactured.

Details: America had abundant supplies of coal, iron ore, petroleum, and copper, along with agricultural products. Technology helped to develop these goods into new useful products. Other developments were: steel replaced iron, a new Atlantic telegraph cable, and the invention of the telephone. The refrigerator car made meatpacking a major industry.

Captains of Industry

Main Idea: In post-Civil War America, power was in the hands of business leaders.

Details: The captain of the steel industry was Andrew Carnegie. John D. Rockefeller owned the Standard Oil Company and was considered a captain of the oil industry. Gustavus Franklin Swift was a leader in meatpacking. Jay Gould became a multi-millionaire in railroading.

Labor Movement

Main Idea: Labor unions formed during the late 1800s because employers showed little interest in the welfare of the workers.

Details: In the 1800s, the National Labor Union, the Knights of Labor, and the Federation of Labor formed. These union organizations fought for better wages, reasonable hours, and safer working conditions.

Jim Crow Laws: Activity (p. 24)

(Answers will vary but may include:)

Central Idea: The South adopted laws targeting African Americans.

Right to Vote

Main idea: Efforts were made to keep black men from voting.

Two Details: Literacy tests, poll taxes, and long periods of residency required; rules passed preventing African Americans from voting in primaries

Jim Crow Laws

Main idea: Jim Crow laws required racial separation.

Two Details: African Americans barred from using white barbershops, theaters, and restaurants; separate schools and state hospitals built for African Americans; separate cars in transportation

Booker T. Washington

Main idea: Booker T. Washington opposed segregation.

Two Details: gave speeches promoting the work ethic and trade education; donated money to overthrow segregation

"Remember the *Maine*": Activity (p. 26)

Event 1: The Venezuelan Boundary Dispute over the boundary between British Guiana and Venezuela had Americans wanting to enforce the Monroe Doctrine.

Event 2: Revolt broke out in Cuba.

Event 3: Newspapers began to feature stories about Spanish atrocities in Cuba.

Event 4: McKinley sent the battleship U.S.S. *Maine* to Havana to protect American property in Cuba. It was destroyed in an explosion.

Theodore Roosevelt Becomes President: Activity (p. 28)

bully pulpit: The presidency gave Roosevelt an opportunity to speak out on issues important to him. He would act on matters even when he had no authority.

square deal: By halting the strike and getting workers a

10 percent increase in pay, both coal miners and owners gained fairly from the agreement.

speak softly and carry a big stick: The nation tried to achieve its aims quietly but was prepared to use force if necessary.

Great White Fleet: The 16 new battleships of the Atlantic Fleet were painted white and sent on a world tour. The fleet was nicknamed the "Great White Fleet."

President William Howard Taft: Activity (p. 30)

1. title, headings, boldface print, illustration, sidebar, caption
2. description or chronological/sequential
3. to inform
4. and 5. Answers will vary.

President Woodrow Wilson: Activity (p. 32)

1. Laws were passed that limited big business and helped the small competitor and worker. Some of these laws were the Underwood Tariff Act that lowered tariffs, the Federal Reserve Act that affected banking, and the Clayton Anti-Trust Act which regulated big business.
2. Germany, Austria-Hungary, Bulgaria, and Turkey
3. England, France, and Russia
4. The United States protested German use of submarine warfare, and the Germans quit for a while. When they resumed in 1917, the United States declared war.

The United States Enters World War I: Activity (p. 34)

Need for Soldiers

Solution: The draft was used for the first time since the Civil War. Men from ages 21 to 30 registered for the draft, but a wider age range of 18 to 45 came later. About 2.8 million men were drafted.

Gaining Support for the War Effort

Solution: Many new agencies were created, such as the Food Administration, War Labor Board, and War Industries Board.

Paying for the War

Solution: The income tax was raised to 4 percent on incomes over $1,000. Money came from "Liberty Loan" drives, and people bought "Liberty Bonds."

Building Patriotic Spirit

Solution: The Creel Committee was created. It put out millions of pamphlets and books and recruited volunteer speakers to drum up support for the war.

Doughboys Are Sent to France: Activity (p. 36)

Who: The main members of the Allied Powers were France, Russia, Britain, and later the United States. The main members of the Central Powers were Germany, Austria-Hungary, Bulgaria, and Turkey.

What: World War I

Where: Europe

When: August 4, 1914 to November 11, 1918

Why: Germany invaded Belgium, then each country's allies joined the war.

Wilson Goes to Versailles: Activity (p. 38)

1. Roosevelt wanted to organize a new Rough Rider unit to go to France. Wilson turned him down.
2. The Irish hated England for refusing to give Ireland its independence.
3. Socialists opposed the war because they saw the war as a way to save capitalism not democracy.
4. Wilson's plan was entitled the Fourteen Points, which called for open diplomacy, freedom of the seas, arms reduction, removal of economic barriers, the return of Alsace-Lorraine to France, an independent Poland, freedom for minorities in Austria-Hungary and Turkey, and an end to the war.

The Treaty of Versailles and the League of Nations: Activity (p. 40)

armistice: a state of peace

treaty: a formally signed agreement between two or more nations

delegate: a representative

league: an alliance of nations with common interests or goals

President Harding's Reputation Is Hurt by Scandals Activity (p. 42)

(Answers will vary, but may include:)

People: two men, one dressed in a business suit and one dressed like a cowboy with a hat

Objects: road sign, steam roller, teapot

Activities: men running in front of the steam roller being pushed by a teapot with steam coming out of spout

Words: Oil Scandal, White House Highway

Inference: The Teapot Dome Scandal leads all the way to the White House. Texas oilmen and business men are trying to run away from their involvement in the Teapot Dome scandal.

The Automobile Changes American Life: Activity (p. 44)

1. The steamer was too slow and complicated, and the electric car was too limited in distance. The Stanley Steamer was too expensive for most people.
2. Electric headlights replaced earlier gaslights, the self-starter prevented arm injuries, and enclosed cars made traveling more comfortable in cold weather.
3. Henry Ford cut the cost of building the Model T by using an assembly line, he painted all cars black, and began making his own parts.
4. Rural areas were no longer isolated, the suburbs grew, and Americans traveled farther from home.

The Stock Market Collapses: Activity (p. 46)

(Answers will vary, but may include:)

1. *Sign:* Farmers were not buying farm equipment.
   Effect: This slowed down the farm implement business.
2. *Sign:* People who had invested in land in Florida in the 1920s had to sell it for whatever price they could get.
   Effect: The loss of money caused them to not want to invest in other ventures.

3. *Sign:* People were too poor to buy radios, washing machines, and new cars.
   Effect: They were not adding to the economy.
4. *Sign:* Many people who had invested in the stock market thought it was too high and took their money out.
   Effect: With fewer people to buy stock, the market began to drop.

Herbert Hoover and the Great Depression: Activity (p. 48)

1. The percentage of state population receiving unemployment relief in 1934
2. South Dakota
3. Delaware, Vermont, Virginia
4. Great Plains region
5. East Coast
6. Answers will vary.

Roosevelt and the New Deal: Activity (p. 50)

(Answers will vary, but may include:)

1. gave FDR expansive control over banks and foreign exchange; insured people's bank deposits
2. cut pay of government employees
3. authorized immediate grants to states for relief projects
4. price controlled agricultural products; paid subsidies to farmers to reduce production of certain crops
5. loaned money to farmers to cover mortgages
6. monitored and regulated stocks and bonds
7. prevented foreclosures on home loans by helping to refinance defaulted home mortgages
8. established Public Works Administration and the National Recovery Administration; gave trade unions right to bargain with employers
9. did not allow commercial banks to be involved with investment business
10. created federal coordinator to oversee joint railroad ventures

The World Is Threatened by Dictators: Activity (p. 52)

<u>Communism in Russia</u>

Key Details: Lenin threatened world revolution; Josef Stalin succeeded Lenin; Communist parties developed in other countries; anti-communists feared loss of property and influence

<u>Fascism in Italy</u>

Key Details: Italy was a poor country; Italian parliament did not deal with growing violence and economic problems; Fascists ready to use force to battle communists; Benito Mussolini appointed premier in 1922, turned into a dictator

<u>Germany and the Third Reich</u>

Key Details: little public support for Weimar Republic; after 1929 communist movement among lower class; Nazi Party led by Adolf Hitler; *Mein Kampf* blamed Germany's problems on Jews; Hitler became Germany's chancellor in 1933; 1934, Hitler named chancellor and president; Hitler's regime called "Third Reich"; set up Jewish concentration camps; 6 million Jews killed by 1945

Military Rule in Japan
Key Details: a population problem in Japan in 1920s; prime minister shot in 1930; military took over government; prepared for war on China

World War II Reaches America: Activity (p. 54)
1935—Italy attacks Ethiopia
1935—Nye Committee report
1936—Spanish Fascists revolt against government
1936—German troops occupy Rhineland
November 1, 1936—Mussolini announces formation of Rome-Berlin Axis
1939—War in Spain ends; Franco in full control
September 1, 1939—war declared on Germany by England and France
December 7, 1941—Pearl Harbor attacked
December 8, 1941—Congress declares war on Japan

The Nation Mobilizes for War: Activity (p. 56)
(Answers will vary, but may include:)
1. The war ended the unemployment problem of the late 1930s. The unemployment in 1944 had dropped to 1.2 percent. Women entered the workforce to fill the jobs previously held by men. Elderly people returned to the workforce in record numbers. Jobs in factories opened their doors to African Americans, who moved from the south to the north or west to find work.
2. Answers will vary.

General Eisenhower Leads the D-Day Invasion: Activity (p. 58)
(Answers will vary, but may include:)
Details: lieutenant colonel; trained tank commanders; served in infantry battalion; traveled to France twice; wrote book on French World War I battlefields; served on assistant secretary of war's staff; served on MacArthur's staff in Philippines; learned to fly; got along with peers which instilled feelings of optimism and trust in his men
Summary: Eisenhower was a lieutenant colonel. He had trained tank commanders. He had served in an infantry battalion, traveled to France twice, and written a book on French World War I battlefields. Eisenhower had served on the assistant secretary of war's staff and on MacArthur's staff in the Philippines. He learned to fly. He got along with his peers and instilled feelings of optimism and trust in his men.

Atomic Blasts End World War II: Activity (p. 60)
1. We are gathered here, representatives of the major warring powers, to conclude a solemn agreement whereby peace may be restored.
2. Let us pray that peace now be restored to the world, and that God will preserve it always. These proceedings are closed.
3. Answers will vary.

The United States Faces New Economic Challenges: Activity (p. 62)
1. People felt Truman was unqualified to serve as president because he had no college education, no foreign policy experience, and no domestic policy-making experience.
2. People needed to replace items like cars, refrigerators, and furniture. Thousands of soldiers, sailors, and marines were returning to civilian life. Unemployment would rise if all of those returning entered the job market at the same time. American producers realized price controls would soon be lifted, and they could get a higher price for their goods. Also, workers were demanding higher wages.
3. Forty days after the United Mine Workers went out on strike, Truman ordered the government to seize the mines. The miners went back to work a week later. When railway workers went out on strike, Truman asked Congress for power to draft workers.

The United States Assumes a World Leader's Role: Activity (p. 64)
United Nations Established
Main Idea: President Roosevelt favored the idea of an international organization to handle disputes before they turned into wars.
Details: United Nations created 1944; made up of a General Assembly (each member one vote) and a Security Council of eleven members (five permanent: United States, England, France, U.S.S.R., and China); each Security Council member had veto power; both Republicans and senators attended the U.N. organizational meetings
Formation of East and West Germany
Main Idea: Actions taken by the United States, Russia, England, and France led to the formation of East and West Germany.
Details: Germany and Austria divided into four zones by Yalta Agreement; Berlin divided into four zones; Russians set up puppet government inside East Germany and Soviet Zone in Austria; 1945, Truman, Churchill and Stalin met at Potsdam to discuss Germany's military and rebuilding of country; 1946, United States, England, and France merge zones and form West Germany; Russia threatens West Berlin; Churchill talks about "iron curtain" descending on Eastern Europe; many Americans concerned about Russia's future intentions
New Agencies are Created
Main Idea: Agencies were restructured or created to advise the president on foreign policy issues.
Details: War and Navy departments merge in 1947 into new Department of Defense; Central Intelligence Agency (CIA) and National Security Council (NSC) formed to advise president on foreign policy matters

The Expansion of Communism in Asia: Activity (p. 66)
(Answers will vary but may include:)
Communists in China
Key Details: United States backs Chinese Nationalists led by Chiang Kai-Shek who fight Mao Zedong's Communists; 1949, Chiang and his army flee to Taiwan; Communist

government in Peking; U.S. does not recognize Peking government; who represents China in United Nations questioned

U.S. Supports South Korea

Key Details: Korea divided at 38th parallel at end of World War II; two separate governments set up; North ally of Russia, South ally of U.S.; June 25, 1950, North Korean troops attack South Korea without warning; Truman does not talk to Congress before sending American air, naval, and land forces to South Korea; attacks condemned by U.N. Security Council; MacArthur appointed to lead U.N. forces in Korea

MacArthur Relieved of His Command

Key Details: MacArthur stabilizes some areas, North Korean troops quickly surrendered; war moved north of 38th parallel; England and France fear China may enter war; MacArthur assures Truman no involvement by China; November 1950, Chinese troops get involved; MacArthur makes public statements about winning war if allowed to do it his way; Truman orders MacArthur to cease public protests, he refuses; April 1951, MacArthur relieved of command by Truman

Summary: There was growing concern over Communist advances in Asia. In China, the United States backed the Chinese Nationalists, led by Chiang Kai-Shek, who was fighting Mao Zedong's Communists. In 1949, Chiang and his army fled to Taiwan. Mao's government sets up in Peking, but the United States refused to recognize it. People wondered who would represent China in the United Nations. After World War II, Korea was divided into two governments: North Korea and South Korea. On June 25, 1950, North Korean troops attacked South Korea without warning. Truman did not consult with Congress before sending American air, naval, and land forces to support South Korea. The U.N. Security Council condemned the attack, and MacArthur was appointed to lead the U.N. forces in Korea. North Korean troops quickly surrendered and the war moved north of the 38th parallel. England and France were afraid China might enter the war, but MacArthur assured Truman that China would not get involved; however, Chinese troops went ahead and crossed the line in November 1950. General MacArthur told the public that he could win the war if he was allowed to do it his way. Truman told MacArthur to cease making public protests, but MacArthur ignored him. In April 1951, President Truman relieved MacArthur of his command.

McCarthyism Sweeps the Nation: Activity (p. 68)

(Answers will vary but may include:)

The Rise of McCarthyism

Details: McCarthy Era, when anyone who had ever joined a communist organization feared exposure, character assassination, loss of income, and disgrace; used fear and frustration to "hunt" American communists

The House Un-American Activities Committee

Details: 1947, looked into accusations against certain members of film industry; Communist Party leader Eugene Dennis charged with conspiring against United States; Julius and Ethel Rosenberg charged with delivering atomic secrets to Russian agents, guilty verdict, executed; 1948, Alger Hiss accused of being Soviet spy

Attacking Communists Makes Headlines

Details: McCarthy attacks communists for headlines; accuses anything suspicious whether guilty or not; accuses General George Marshall, General Dwight Eisenhower, Senator Millard Tydings, Secretary of State Dean Acheson, Dr. J. Robert Oppenheimer, Protestant ministers, U.S. Information Agency, some in executive branch who refuse to turn over classified documents

The Senate Censures McCarthy

Details: Army challenges McCarthy charges; televised hearings held; McCarthy looks like arrogant bully; December 1954, Senate censures McCarthy

Desegregation in America: Activity (p. 70)

1. The Supreme Court decision denounced segregation in schools. The border states began desegregating.
2. An African-American group in Montgomery, Alabama, organized a city-wide bus boycott. Martin Luther King, Jr., was the leader.
3. The Civil Rights Act of 1957 authorized the Department of Justice to prosecute any official who denied African Americans the right to vote.

The Cuban Missile Crisis: Activity (p. 72)

(Answers will vary, but may include:)

U-2 Spy Plane Incident

Key Details: tension between United States and U.S.S.R.; May 1, 1960, American U-2 spy plane shot down in Soviet territory; pilot captured; U.S. denies it was spying; Khrushchev asks U.S. for apology; Eisenhower refuses to apologize; Khrushchev left the summit.

Summary: There was tension between the United States and the U.S.S.R. The tension was not helped when an American U-2 spy plane was shot down in Soviet territory on May 1, 1960, and the pilot was captured. Khrushchev asked the United States to apologize for spying on the Soviet Union. President Eisenhower refused to apologize. Khrushchev left the summit.

Cuban Missile Crisis

Key Details: U-2 flies over Cuba and sees missile launch pads; Kennedy responds by saying U.S. ships would stop any Russian ship carrying missiles; Khrushchev backs down; missiles in Cuba returned to Russia; United States promises to never invade Cuba in future

Summary: An American U-2 spy plane discovered missile launch pads had been built in Cuba. President Kennedy responded by announcing U.S. ships would stop any Russian ships that appeared to be carrying missiles. Soviet Leader Khrushchev backed down, and the missiles in Cuba were returned to Russia. The United States promised to never invade Cuba in the future.

The Vietnam War: Activity (p. 74)
(Answers will vary, but may include:)
1. In order to promote and keep the peace world-wide and keep Southeast Asia secure
2. Vietnamese naval units violated the Charter of the United Nations and international law by attacking U.S. vessels, which were lawfully in international waters. This action has threatened international peace.
3. The attacks were part of a plan created by the Communist regime in North Vietnam against its neighbors and the countries that supported them.
4. The U. S. does not want to take over the land, military, or governments of Southeast Asia. Their only desire is to help Southeast Asians who want to be free and live in peace.
5. Congress approves all actions taken by the President as Commander in Chief in order to repel any armed attack against the U.S. and to prevent future attacks.

1968—A Tragic Year: Activity (p. 76)
(Teacher verification is required.)

President Richard Nixon and Watergate: Activity (p. 78)
(Answers will vary but may include:)
1. President Nixon reduced the U.S. military force in Vietnam to 50,000. He and his chief foreign policy advisor, Henry Kissinger, worked toward a relaxing of tension between the United States and the U.S.S.R. He opened diplomatic relations with communist China and visited Chairman Mao in Peking. He pushed for two new agencies, the Environmental Protection Agency (EPA) and the Occupational Safety and Health Administration (OSHA). He approved increasing social security benefits, a reform of the tax system, and federal aid to low- and middle-income home buyers. To boost the economy, he put on price and wage controls.
2. Five burglars were caught breaking into the Democratic headquarters at the Watergate complex in Washington. Nixon won the 1972 presidential election. The burglars were sentenced to 20 years in prison. One of the burglars told the judge that higher officials in the Committee to Reelect the President were involved. Two *Washington Post* reporters were fed information about a cover-up from a secret source. A Senate committee began an investigation and a special prosecutor was appointed. A lawyer for Nixon admitted to attending White House meetings where a cover-up was discussed. Nixon denied any wrongdoing. It was discovered that Nixon taped discussions in the Oval Office. The special prosecutor tried to get the tapes but was fired and a new prosecutor was appointed. The Supreme Court ordered Nixon to turn over the tapes. The House Judiciary Committee voted three charges of impeachment. Senate Republican leaders went to Nixon and asked him to resign, which Nixon did on August 9, 1974.

Celebration of the American Dream: Activity (p. 80)
(Teacher verification is required.)

President Ronald Reagan: Activity (p. 82)
(Teacher verification is required.)

A New Millennium: Activity (p. 84)
Threat of Y2K
Key Details: people feared malfunction of computers on 01/01/2000; programmers created a Y2K bug fix; very few problems reported on 01/01/2000
Hope for Peace
Key Details: communism fell apart; Soviet Union broken apart into independent countries; Berlin Wall torn down; 1991, Persian Gulf War; peacekeeping missions during Clinton administration
Unrest Grows in the Middle East
Key Details: assassinations and terrorist bombings in Israel and Palestinian-controlled lands and African nations; world leaders work toward peace in Middle East
Terrorism at Home
Key Details: federal building in Oklahoma bombed by home-grown terrorists; 168 killed

A National Tragedy—September 11, 2001: Activity (p. 86)
(Teacher verification is required.)

President Barack Obama: Activity (p. 88)
August 27, 2008—became Democratic Party's presidential nominee
November 4, 2008—elected President of the U.S.
January 20, 2009—inauguration day
February 17, 2009—signed ARRA
March 23, 2010—signed Affordable Care Act
July 21, 2010—signed Dodd-Frank
February 2, 2011—signed New START Treaty
May 2, 2011—approved raid on and killing of Osama bin Laden
November 6, 2012—reelected to second term
July 2015—Iran Nuclear Deal
October 2015—unemployment rate dropped to 5%
December 2015—announced 13.7 million new jobs

Photo Credit:
pg. 14 Chinese railroad workers sierra nevada.jpg {PD-Old} Joseph Becker, illustrator. *Frank Leslie's Illustrated Newspaper.* 6 Feb. 1870. Nagualdesign. 26 Jul. 2016. <https://commons.wikimedia.org/wiki/File:Chinese_railroad_workers_sierra_nevadas.jpg>